PRAISE FOR PREVIOUS EKPHRASTIC BOOKS BY JOSEPH STANTON

Praise for *Imaginary Museum: Poems on Art*

"Countless poets have felt called upon to write poems to and about their favorite painting. But I know of no other volume that has undertaken as ambitious a course as Joseph Stanton's *Imaginary Museum*, a veritable Prado of Poems. It is most attractive in its completeness and, at the same time, in its loving concentration on individual paintings. It is a work deserving of repeated visits."

— THEODORE WEISS, editor of *Quarterly Review of Literature*

"It is a great joy to meet so many beloved paintings by Bruegel, Hopper, Rousseau, Vermeer, Magritte, and others gathered under the same imaginary roof, and to follow a guide so sensible to aesthetic signs, so gifted for reading the canvases into poetic language. Joseph Stanton's collection ought to be found in every art gallery shop and in every classroom where relations between word and image are lectured and discussed."

— HANS LUND, professor of comparative literature, Lund University, Sweden

"Joseph Stanton's poems on art exhibit a subtle collaboration with the artist. His poems on pictures convey a narrative inspired by, not imposed upon, the visible stories. They are poems of mood and meditation, and they make you want to look at the paintings again and read these wonderful poems again and again."

— TONY QUAGLIANO, author of *Language Matters*

"Joseph Stanton has organized this outstanding collection . . . as if it were a museum tour. He enters the space of artifact after artifact, filling his poems with story. . . . Stanton's skillful handling of poems about art should come as no surprise. He has studied and written extensively about the aesthetics of the ekphrastic stance — working out in theory what actually takes place when a poet writes a poem about an art piece. *Imaginary Museum* is not, however, a book of theory. It is a stunning collection of lyrical poetry. . . . What rises over the full range of these poems is the clear, lyric voice of a masterful ekphrastic poet."

— Laverne and Carol Frith, editors of *Ekphrasis*

"In galleries of this imaginary museum, the elegant figures painted on a Greek amphora and the long forgotten souls of ladies and soldiers of Noh theatre speak out their hidden dreams in their own way. They even tell us their hopes and their revived dreams. This is a world of savage bloody scenes mingled with serene celestial griefs. Joseph Stanton portrays this other world with deep insight and delicate expression, until this other world begins to hear its own name."

— Ōoka Makota, author of *Beneath the Sleepless Tossing of the Planets: Selected Poems*

Praise for *Things Seen*

"Poet Joseph Stanton puts me in mind of those Chinese court literati of the Ming and Sung dynasties who were not simply scholars, but were also expected to compose and recite poetry and to be connoisseurs and philosophers of art, of all arts. What a range is in these one hundred pages, reflecting interests he has long explored in his work, from the questions of what an artist sees and how a painting or art object means, to the moonlit and irredeemably haunted landscape of Noh drama, to the atmosphere and timeless moments of the game of baseball. And what diverse artists he has accompanied into their works — Gauguin, Gorey, Zeshin — giving his attention and language to what they see and what he sees so that we might see too. He devotes one whole section to the life and vision of an old favorite, Edward Hopper. "Mostly Grimm" — poems based on well- and lesser-known tales — is well named, because Stanton's often playful reimagining refreshes the classic themes and images. Although Stanton has often written directly about baseball, the poems of the final section, "Painting the Corners," are particularly interesting because of their several layers and removes. Here the poet/artist notices how the artist sees as he in turn captures fleeting scenes from the art of baseball. Poet and artist have become inseparable in this collection."

— Sue Cowing, author of *Call Me Drog*

"Joseph Stanton is a poet of the visual. He willingly and often joyously assumes the ekphrastic stance, his poems moving seamlessly from an interpretation of Paul Gauguin's powerful *Vision After the Sermon,* in which Jacob grapples with an angel, to a series of poems exploring the alienated world of the twentieth century painter Edward Hopper with its emerging complexities and its journey into the dichotomies of the urban and the rural, the internal and the external. Through the revelatory lens of *Things Seen*, Stanton observes the Noh theater tradition, analyzes the Brothers Grimm, and finalizes the collection with a series of observations about baseball as interpreted by paintings, his focus on America's favorite pastime illustrated with an exciting series of engagements. As eclectic as his varied subject matter may be, the basic theme of these meticulously wrought poems remains the same — vision — the act of creative seeing. In the 'Noh Variations' poem 'Aya no Tsuzumi,' he writes, 'I have spent my soul/on a glimpse of moon/through bare branches.' This richly visual collection turns on Stanton's masterful transliteration of image after image into the essence of its own perceived light."

— LAVERNE AND CAROL FRITH, editors of *Ekphrasis*

"Joseph Stanton's tone knows his own 'deft, ungraspable self.' The wit in this last line from a poem about Gauguin's *Vision After the Sermon*, washes through *Things Seen* with the humility, intelligence and will to have serious fun with famous art — paintings, Grimm tales, noh plays — treated as living experience."

— PAUL NELSON, author of *Burning the Furniture*

"Joseph Stanton's *Things Seen* is one of the great books of poetry this year that probably will not get the attention it deserves, though I hope my sheer delight might conspire otherwise. His is a major voice and these poems artifacts of an exquisite musical craftsman possessed of a generosity of vision and a special quality of attention that transforms art into being. As the poem about Paul Gauguin's *Vision After the Sermon* offers us, "a roseate window" in which the story "gleams for all to see; / my struggle to know, my difficult wrestling / with that indefatigable god—/ my deft, ungraspable self." *Things Seen* is divided into five discrete sections—ekphrasis that gives fresh insight into that timeless practice; reinventions of fairy tales that remake the Prince Frog, The Fir Apple, Godfather Death, and leave us the Shepherd Boy to calculate the universe; Noh variations that demonstrate why that word is derived from the Japanese word for "skill"; a series on Edward Hopper that intertwines his art and life; and deft poems about paintings about baseball — and yet by the end the sections feel as triumphantly cohesive as the movements in a symphony. *Things Seen* offers us the poet at the height of perception and the skills of conjuration."

— Ravi Shakar, author of *What Else Could It Be*

Moving Pictures

Moving Pictures

poems by

Joseph Stanton

Shanti Arts Publishing
Brunswick, Maine

MOVING PICTURES

Published by Shanti Arts Publishing
Designed by Shanti Arts Designs

Shanti Arts LLC
193 Hillside Road
Brunswick, Maine 04011
shantiarts.com

Printed in the United States of America

ISBN: 978-1-947067-85-1 (softcover)

Library of Congress Control Number: 2019940587

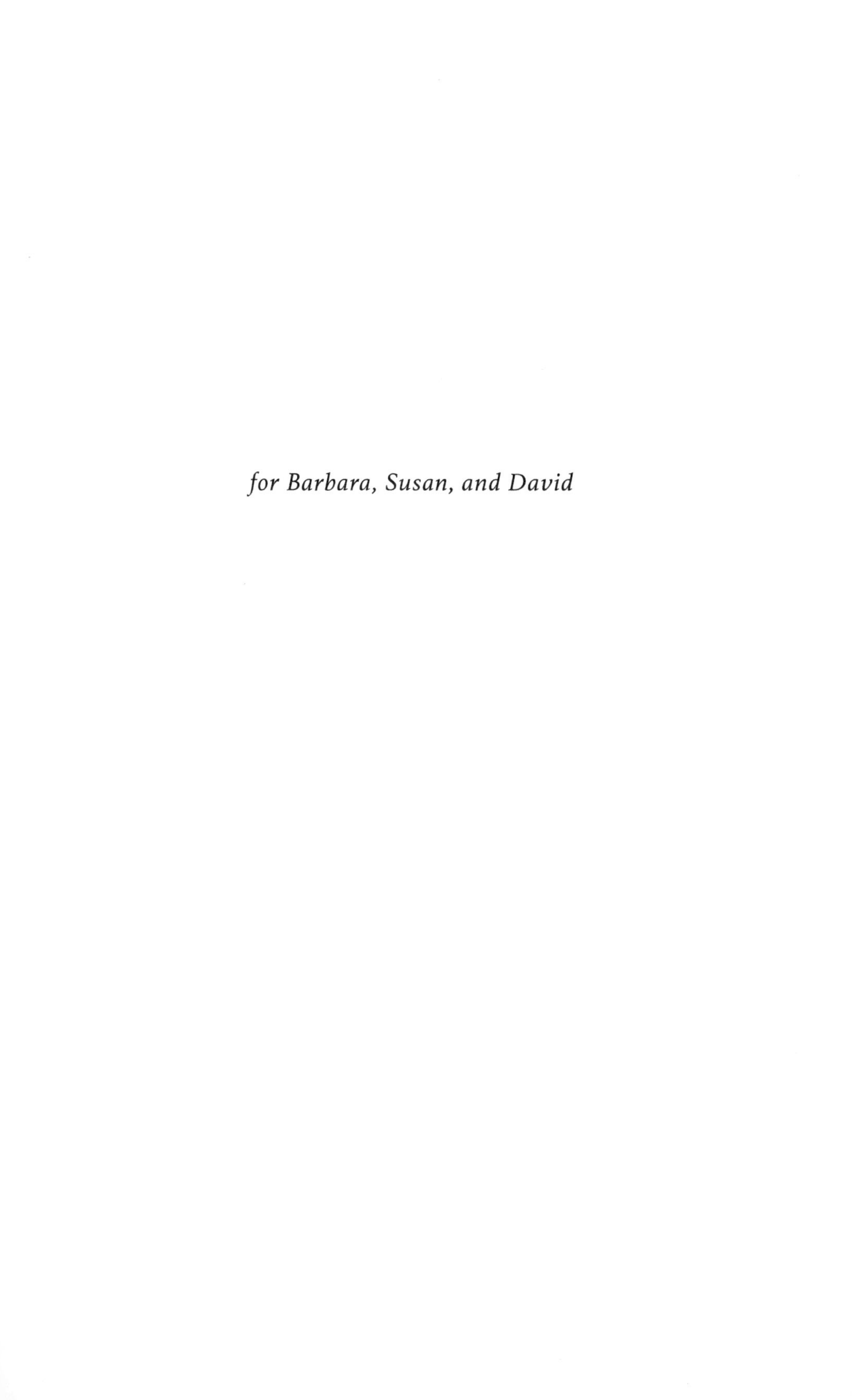

for Barbara, Susan, and David

Contents

Painting the Corners

Image Information

Due to copyright restrictions, not all images referenced in the poems are pictured, but the information below will assist in viewing them online or in person.

[29] Piero di Cosimo, *Saint John the Evangelist*, 1504. Oil on panel. Honolulu Museum of Art, Honolulu, Hawai'i. WC PD

[31] Giambologna, *Rape of a Sabine Woman*, 1581–83. Loggia dei Lanzi, Florence, Italy. Photograph by saiko, 2012. WC CC

[34] Pieter de Hooch, *A Musical Conversation*, 1674. Oil. Honolulu Museum of Art, Honolulu, Hawai'i. WC PD

[36] Alexandre Cabanel, *Echo*, 1874. Oil on canvas. 38.5 x 26.2 inches (97.8 x 66.7 cm). Metropolitan Museum of Art, New York City, New York. WC PD

[38] Paul Gauguin, *Two Nudes on a Tahitian Beach*, 1892. Oil on canvas. 35.7 x 25.5 inches (90.8 x 64.8 cm). Honolulu Museum of Art, Honolulu, Hawai'i. WC PD

[40] Vincent van Gogh, *Wheat Field*, 1888. Oil on canvas. 21.7 x 26.2 inches (66.2 x 66.6 cm). Honolulu Museum of Art, Honolulu, Hawai'i. WC PD

[44] Gustave Caillebotte, *Mademoiselle Boissière Knitting*, 1877. Oil on canvas. 25.6 x 31.4 inches (65.1 x 80.0 cm). Museum of Fine Arts, Houston, Texas. WC PD

[46] Umberto Boccioni, *States of Mind I: The Farewells*, 1911. Oil on canvas. 27.7 x 37.8 inches (70.5 x 96.2 cm). Museum of Modern Art, New York City, New York. WC PD

[48] Paul Klee, *Twittering Machine*, 1922. Oil transfer drawing, watercolor, and ink on paper with gouache and ink borders on board. 25.2 x 19.0 inches (64.1 x 48.3 cm). Museum of Modern Art, New York City, New York. WC PD

[50] René Magritte, *The Unexpected Answer*, 1933. Oil on canvas. Magritte Museum, Brussels, Belguim. (not pictured)

[52] René Magritte, *When Evening Falls*, 1964. Oil on canvas. 63.2 x 44.8 inches (160.5 x 113.5 cm). Private collection. (not pictured)

[53] René Magritte, *Infinite Reconnaissance,* 1933. Oil on canvas. 39.3 x 28.7 inches (97.5 x 73.0 cm). Private collection. (not pictured)

[56] United States Geological Survey, New York: Kaaterskill Quadrangle, 1903. Princeton University Library, Princeton, New Jersey. PD

[59] Thomas Cole, *A View of the Mountain Pass Called the Notch of the White Mountains (Crawford Notch)*, 1839. Oil on canvas. 40.1 x 61.3 inches (102.0 x 155.8 cm). National Gallery of Art, Washington D.C. WC PD

[61] Thomas Cole, *The Voyage of Life: Childhood*, 1842. Oil on canvas. 52.8 x 76.8 inches (134.3 x 195.3 cm). National Gallery of Art, Washington D.C. WC PD

[61] Thomas Cole, *The Voyage of Life: Youth*, 1842. Oil on canvas. 52.8 x 76.8 inches (134.3 x 195.3 cm). National Gallery of Art, Washington D.C. WC PD

[63] Thomas Cole, *The Voyage of Life: Manhood*, 1842. Oil on canvas. 52.8 x 76.8 inches (134.3 x 195.3 cm). National Gallery of Art, Washington D.C. WC PD

[63] Thomas Cole, *The Voyage of Life: Old Age*, 1842. Oil on canvas. 52.8 x 76.8 inches (134.3 x 195.3 cm). National Gallery of Art, Washington D.C. WC PD

[69] Frederic Edwin Church, *Andes of the Ecuador*, 1855. Oil. Honolulu Museum of Art, Honolulu, Hawai'i. WC PD

[71] Raphaelle Peale, *Still Life with Oranges*, 1818. Oil on wood panel. 18.6 x 22.9 inches (47.4 x 58.3 cm). Toledo Museum of Art, Toledo, Ohio. WC PD

[72] Winslow Homer, *Snap the Whip*, 1872. Oil on canvas. 22.0 x 35.9 inches (56.0 x 91.4 cm). Butler Institute of American Art, Youngstown, Ohio. WC PD (also pictured on front cover)

[75] Winslow Homer, *Moonlight*, 1874. Watercolor and gouache on paper. Arkell Museum, Canajoharie, New York. WC PD

[77] Winslow Homer, *Sunset Fires*, 1880. Watercolor on paper. 9.7 x 13.6 inches (24.7 x 34.6 cm). The Westmoreland Museum of American Art, Greensburg, Pennsylvania. WC PD

[78] Winslow Homer, *The Adirondack Guide*, 1894. Watercolor

over graphite on paper. 15.1 x 21.4 inches (38.5 x 54.6 cm). Museum of Fine Arts, Boston, Massachusetts. WC PD

[81] Winslow Homer, *An October Day*, 1889. Watercolor over graphite on paper. 14.0 x 19.7 inches (35.7 x 50.2 cm). Clark Art Institute, Williamstown, Massachusetts. WC PD

[82] Winslow Homer, *Inside the Bar*, 1883. Watercolor and graphite on paper. 15.9 x 29.0 inches (40.6 x 73.7). Metropolitan Museum of Art, New York City, New York. WC PD

[85] Winslow Homer, *Sunlight on the Coast*, 1890. Oil on canvas. 30.2 x 48.5 inches (76.9 x 123.3 cm). Toledo Museum of Art, Toledo, Ohio. WC PD

[87] Joseph Stella, *Brooklyn Bridge*, 1919–20. Oil on canvas. 84.7 x 76.6 inches (215.3 x 194.6 cm). Yale University Art Gallery, New Haven, Connecticut. WC PD

[88] Edward Hopper, *Route 6, Eastham*, 1941. Oil on canvas. Swope Art Museum, Terre Haute, Indiana. (not pictured)

[89] Edward Hopper, *Freight Cars, Gloucester*, 1928. Oil on canvas. 29.0 x 40.1 inches (73.7 x 101.9 cm). Addison Gallery of American Art, Phillips Academy, Andover, Massachusetts. (not pictured)

[90] Edward Hopper, *The City*, 1927. Oil on canvas. 36.9 x 27.4 inches (93.9 x 69.8 cm). Private collection. (not pictured)

[91] Edward Hopper, *Room in New York*, 1934. Oil on canvas. 29.1 x 36.6 inches (73.9 x 92.9 cm). Sheldon Museum of Art, University of Nebraska–Lincoln. (not pictured)

[92] Edward Hopper, *Summer Evening*, 1947. Oil on canvas. Private collection. (not pictured)

[93] Edward Hopper, *Stairway*, 1949. Oil on wood. 16.0 x 11.8 inches (40.6 x 30.2 cm). Whitney Museum of American Art, New York City, New York. (not pictured)

[94] Edward Hopper, *Haunted House*, 1926. Watercolor on paper. 14.0 x 20.0 inches (35.5 x 50.8 cm). Farnsworth Art Museum, Rockland, Maine. (not pictured)

[95] Edward Hopper, *House of the Foghorn*, 1927. Watercolor,

gouache, and charcoal on paper. 13.8 x 20.0 inches (35.2 x 50.8 cm). Metropolitan Museum of Art, New York City, New York. (not pictured)

[96] Edward Hopper, *On the Quai: The Suicide*, 1907. Conté, wash and touches of white. 17.5 x 14.0 inches (44.5 x 37.1 cm). Private collection. (not pictured)

[97] Edward Hopper, *Two Comedians*, 1965. Oil on canvas. 29 x 40 inches (73.7 x 101.6 cm). Private collection. (not pictured)

[98] Edward Hopper, *A Woman in the Sun*, 1961. Oil on linen. 40.1 x 60.3 inches (101.9 x 152.9 cm). Whitney Museum of American Art, New York City, New York. (not pictured)

[99] Giovanni Bellini, *Saint Francis in the Desert*, c. 1480. Oil and tempera on poplar wood. 48.9 x 55.5 inches (124.4 x 141.0 cm). The Frick Collection, New York City, New York. WC PD

[101] Ansel Adams, *Moonrise, Hernandez, New Mexico*, 1941. Gelatin silver print. 15.7 x 19.5 inches (40.0 x 49.5 cm). Museum of Modern Art, New York City, New York. (not pictured)

[102] Isamu Noguchi, *To Love*, 1970–71. Portuguese Rose Aurora marble and black Austrian Porticoi marble. 11.1 x 14.8 x 22.3 inches (28.3 x 37.8 x 56.8 cm). Noguchi Museum, Long Island City, New York. (not pictured)

[103] Edward Gorey, *The Fantod Pack*, first published in 1995 by Gotham Book Mart in a limited edition. (not pictured)

[104] H. C. Westermann, *Nouveau Rat Trap*, 1965. Birch plywood, rosewood, metal, and rubber bumpers. Honolulu Museum of Art, Honolulu, Hawai‘i. (not pictured)

[105] Yoko Ono, *A Hole to See the Sky Through*, 1971. Announcement postcard for a Yoko Ono show. 3.7 x 5.7 inches (9.6 x 14.5 cm). (not pictured)

[108] Deryl Daniel Mackie, *Smokey Joe Williams*, 1985. National Baseball Hall of Fame, Cooperstown, New York. (not pictured)

[111] Tim Swartz, *Stretching II*, 1990. Watercolor on paper. 22 x 30 inches (56 x 76 cm). Used with permission of the artist.

[112] Ben Shahn, *Vacant Lot*, 1939. Watercolor and gouache on paper mounted on panel. 19 x 23 inches (48.2 x 58.4 cm). Wadsworth Atheneum, Hartford, Connecticut. (not pictured)

[114] Robert Riggs, *The Impossible Play*, 1949. Tempera on panel. 10.7 x 31.5 inches (80.0 x 27.3 cm). Private collection. (not pictured)

[116] Jacob Lawrence, *Strike*, 1949. Tempera. 20 x 24 inches (50.8 x 60.9 cm). Private collection. (not pictured)

[119] Lisa Dinhofer, *Spring Street Hardball*, 1988. Oil on linen. 40 x 25 inches (101.6 x 63.5 cm). Gladstone Collection of Baseball Art. Used with permission of the artist.

[120] Andy Warhol, *Baseball*, 1962. Silkscreen on canvas. 82.0 x 91.5 inches (208.2 x 232.4 cm). Nelson-Atkins Museum of Art, Kansas City, Missouri. (not pictured)

[122] Andy Warhol, *Pete Rose,* 1985. Screenprint. 31.5 x 39.4 inches (80.0 x 99.9 cm). National Portrait Gallery, Washington D. C. (not pictured)

[123] Seymour Leichman, *Fate Takes a Hand,* 1969. Lithograph. 29.5 x 22.0 inches (74.9 x 55.8 cm). Private collection. (not pictured)

[125] *Jackie Robinson Steals Home Against the Chicago Cubs in 1952*. National Baseball Hall of Fame and Museum, Cooperstown, New York. Used with permission.

[129] Ingrid Bergman and Humphrey Bogart in *Casablanca*, 1942. Screenshot. WC PD

[142] Ava Gardner and Burt Lancaster in *The Killers,* 1946. Screenshot. WC PD

WC: Wikimedia Commons
PD: Public Domain
CC: Creative Commons License

Acknowledgments

The author would like to thank the editors of these publications in which the following poems have appeared, often in different versions:

Aethlon, "Deryl Mackie's *Smokey Joe Williams*" and "Jacob Lawrence's *Strike*" • ***Blueline***, "Winslow Homer's *Adirondack Guide*" and "Winslow Homer's *An October Day*" • ***Chaminade Literary Review,*** "'We'll Always Have Paris': Years Later, Rick Thinks He Sees Ilsa, One Last Time, in Paris" • ***The Cortland Review,*** "Storm at Cedarmere" • ***Ekphrasis,*** "Gustave Caillebotte's *Madame Boissière Knitting*," "Paul Klee's *Twittering Machine*," "*The Seventh Seal*," "Thomas Cole's *Notch of the White Mountains*," "Thomas Cole's *The Voyage of Life*," "Winslow Homer's *Moonlight*," "Winslow Homer's *Snap the Whip*," "Winslow Homer's *Sunlight on the Coast*," and "Winslow Homer's *Sunset Fires*" • ***Ekphrastic Review***, "Edward Hopper's *Room in New York*," "Joseph Stella's *Brooklyn Bridge*," "Piero di Cosimo's *Saint John*," "Raphaelle Peale's *Still Life with Oranges*," "René Magritte's *Infinite Recognition*," and "René Magritte's *The Unexpected Answer*" • ***Long Island Quarterly,*** "Pond at Cedarmere" and "The Usual Suspects" • ***Poetry Bay,*** "*Eternal Sunshine of the Spotless Mind*," "*The Killers*," and "On a Classic Photo of *Jackie Robinson Stealing Home*" • ***13 Miles from Cleveland,*** "*Groundhog Day*" and "*Vertigo*" • ***Spitball,*** "Andy Warhol's *Baseball*," "Andy Warhol's *Pete Rose*," and "Tim Swartz's *Stretching*" • ***Sport Literate,*** "Seymour Leichman's *Fate Takes a Hand*"

Seeing Things, European Wing

The Origins of European Painting

In one sort of beginning the gold leaf behind
the martyrs and madonnas breaks down into

the gold deserts of Gherardo di Jacopo Starnina
where jagged rocks pretend to be mountains,

and saints multiply into multitudes of monks
scurrying here and there in a holy congestion,

oddly suggestive of Midtown Manhattan.

Piero di Cosimo's *Saint John*

This Evangelist is a paradox.
His face — so gentle,
so benign,
transcendent with love of God

and mankind, too —
belies his powerful hands,
muscular of palm,
thick of wrist.

These are the hands of a man
you would not want
to wrestle with,
but, strangely,

they are also
the hands of a saint so pure
he persuades poison
to depart as snake.

They are, we also know,
the hands of Christ's best friend
who sticks with his Jesus
to the bitterest of ends.

And these are the hands,
that will, at the last,
craft the fiercely lovely poetry,
the words that will be

revelations.

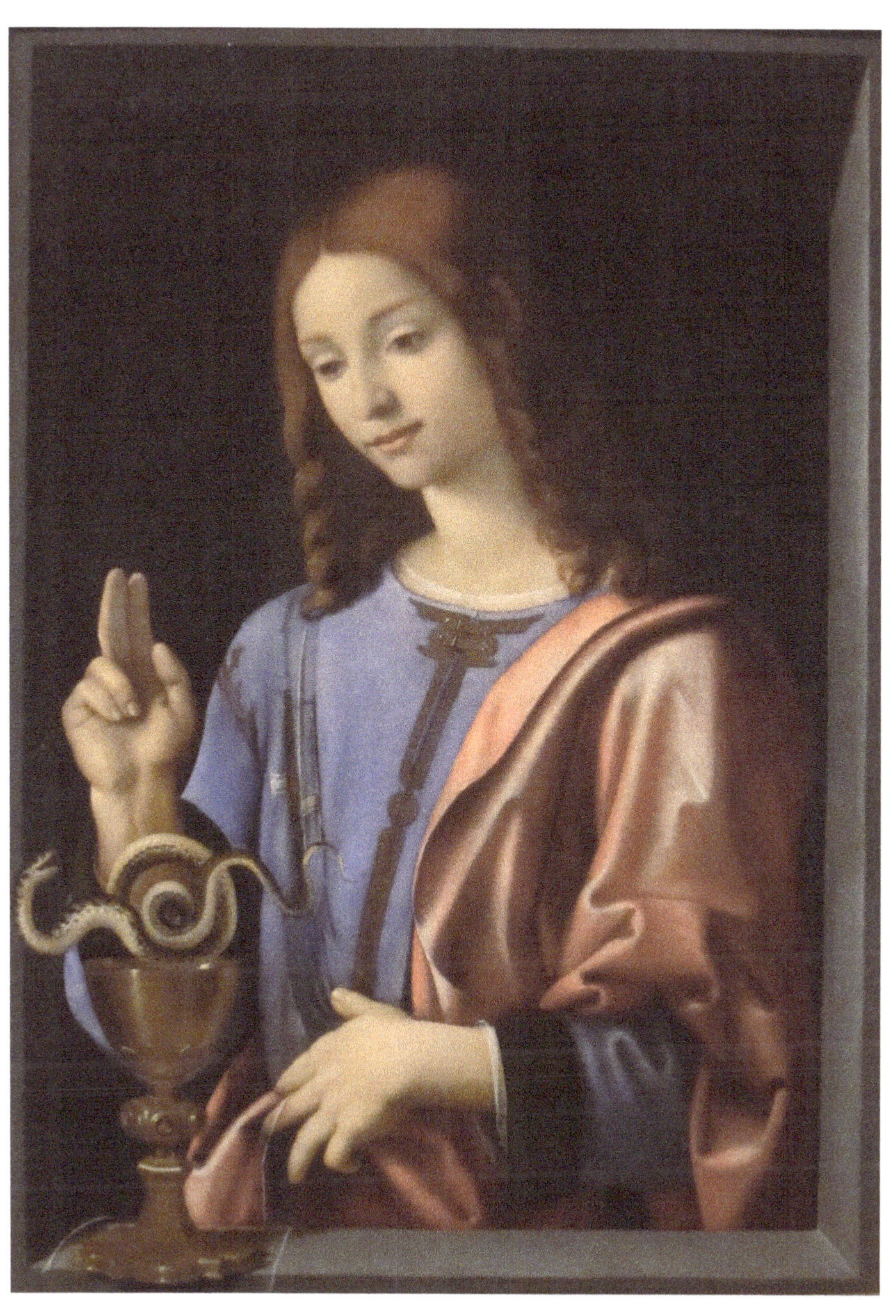

Piero di Cosimo, *Saint John the Evangelist*, 1504

Giambologna's
Rape of a Sabine Woman

This most remarkable
of monumental Mannerist marbles,
gives rape a distinctive twist.

Round and round they go —
the captured woman twists
upwards towards an arch

of Firenzi's Loggia dei Lanzi,
carried aloft by her cruel captor,
who has stepped over

the crouching older man,
the woman's father,
whose horrified upward gaze

locks eyes with his daughter's
desperate downward plea.
It's the same old story,

(continued)

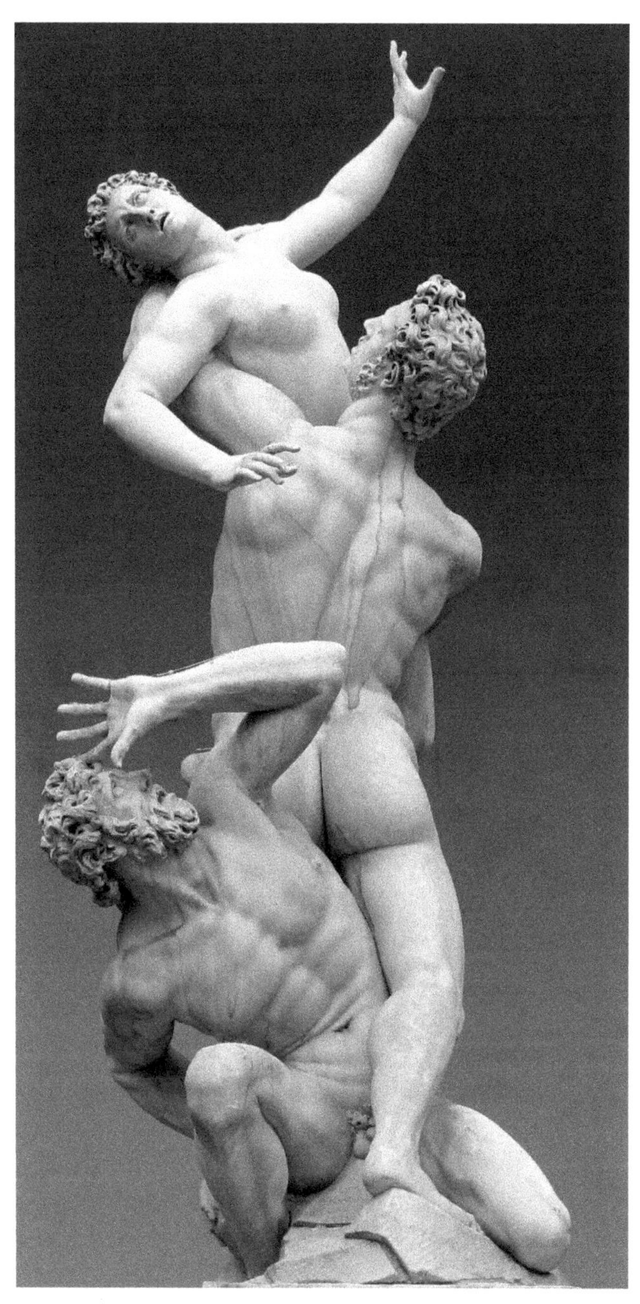

Giambologna, *Rape of a Sabine Woman*, 1581–83

this lustful fighting,
this grasping after
the unjustifiable,

this spectacular
polar opposite
of the golden rule.

Formally,
it is the ultimate
in skillfully rendering:

three perfectly modeled bodies,
intertwined
in a balanced verticality,

a beautifully undercut
exposure of the inhumanity
of humanity.

Pieter de Hooch's *A Musical Conversation*

De Hooch's conversation
involves two sets of lovers,
the instruments the painter plays upon.
We can presume the music is baroque,
counterpointed for four, a quartet of sorts,
on the cello of the central woman;

on the mandolin of the right-hand man,
who is tuning his strings in preparation;
on the voice of the woman,
who holds the song book by the window
at an angle to allow her lover, the fourth instrument,
to sing it over her shoulder,

distracted though he is
by her décolletage
that blocks, attractively, his view.
She seems already to be humming
the chosen tune,
a song we can wager is a song of love.

(continued)

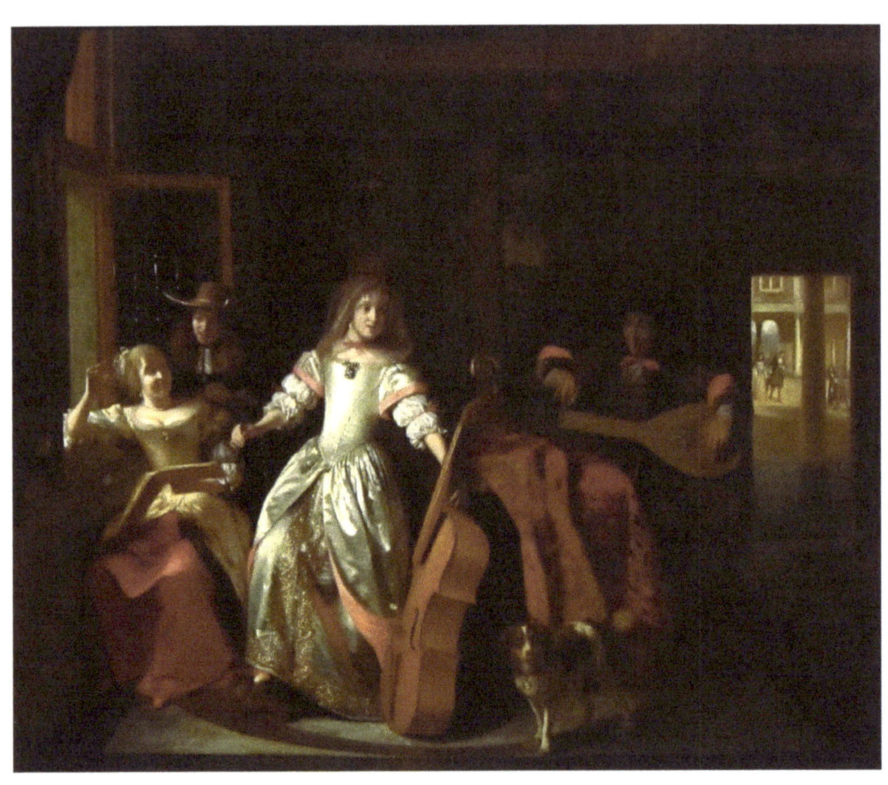

Pieter de Hooch, *A Musical Conversation*, 1674

This musical conversation
makes light of dark, dark of light —
a chiaroscuro that plays a fugue of colors,
an aria about affection and its aftermath.
At the feet of the lovers a dog,
symbol of fidelity, wags its tail

(perhaps not ironically),
and we can glimpse through a doorway
in the distance, in full light,
another set of lovers engaged in bowing.
Their more distanced loving might be
a conversation of dancing.

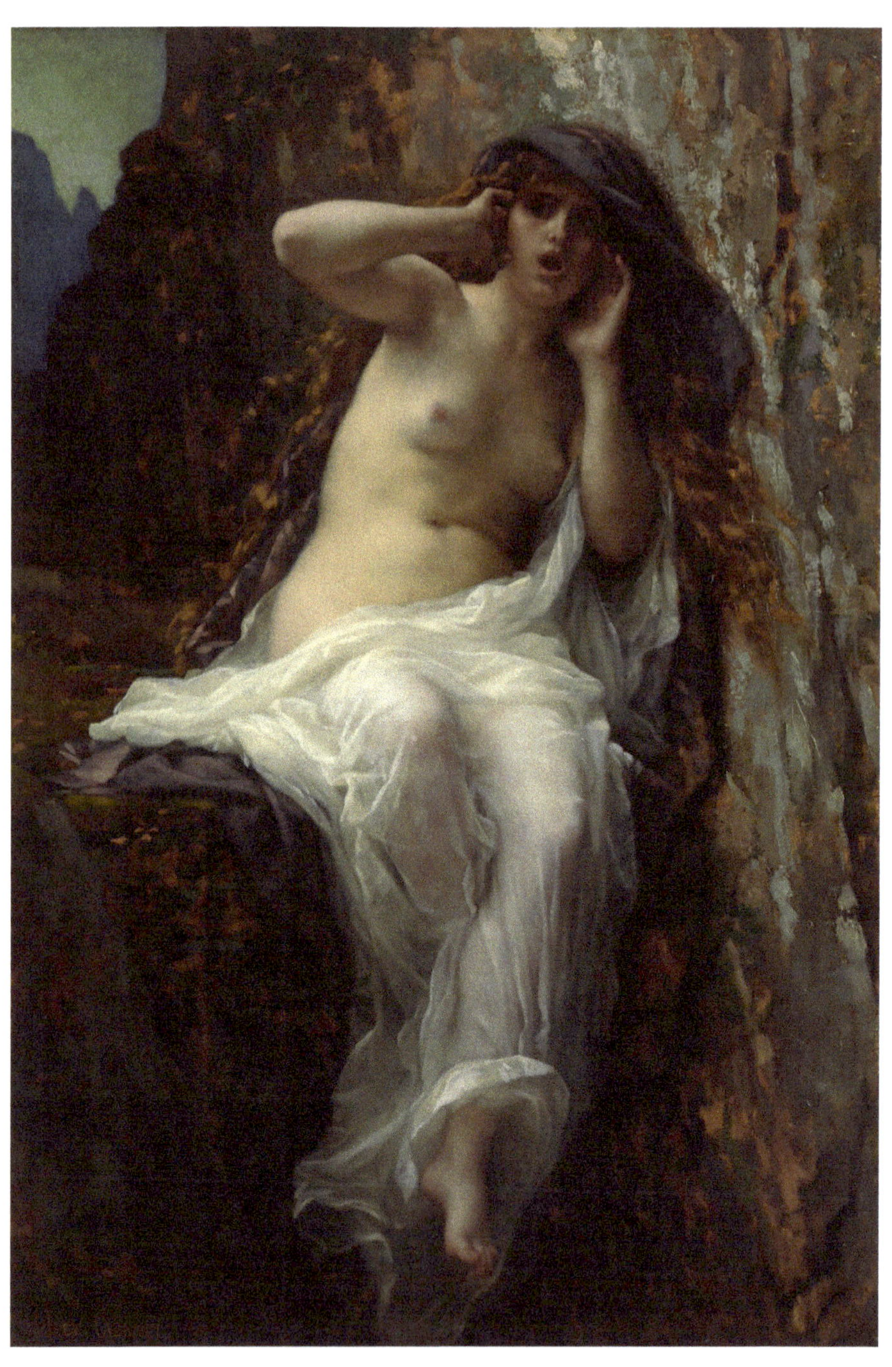

Alexandre Cabanel, *Echo*, 1874

Alexander Cabanel's *Echo*

Words she dearly wanted to say,
to tell him she loved him with all her heart,
were echoes only and he would not stay.

He was the sun that lights her day.
From him she hoped never to part.
There were words she wanted to say.

Cursed to repeat, it was her only way
to speak the deep deep love she thought,
but echoes could not make him stay.

At last she ran to him in full dismay,
but in her love he would take no part
nor hear the words her echoes tried to say.

His love was all for his own face.
Narcissus had himself only at heart.
An echo could not make him stay.

Narcissus wasted down to nothing day by day,
while Echo's voice lingered lost and desolate.
There were words she dearly wanted to say,
but echoes could not make him stay.

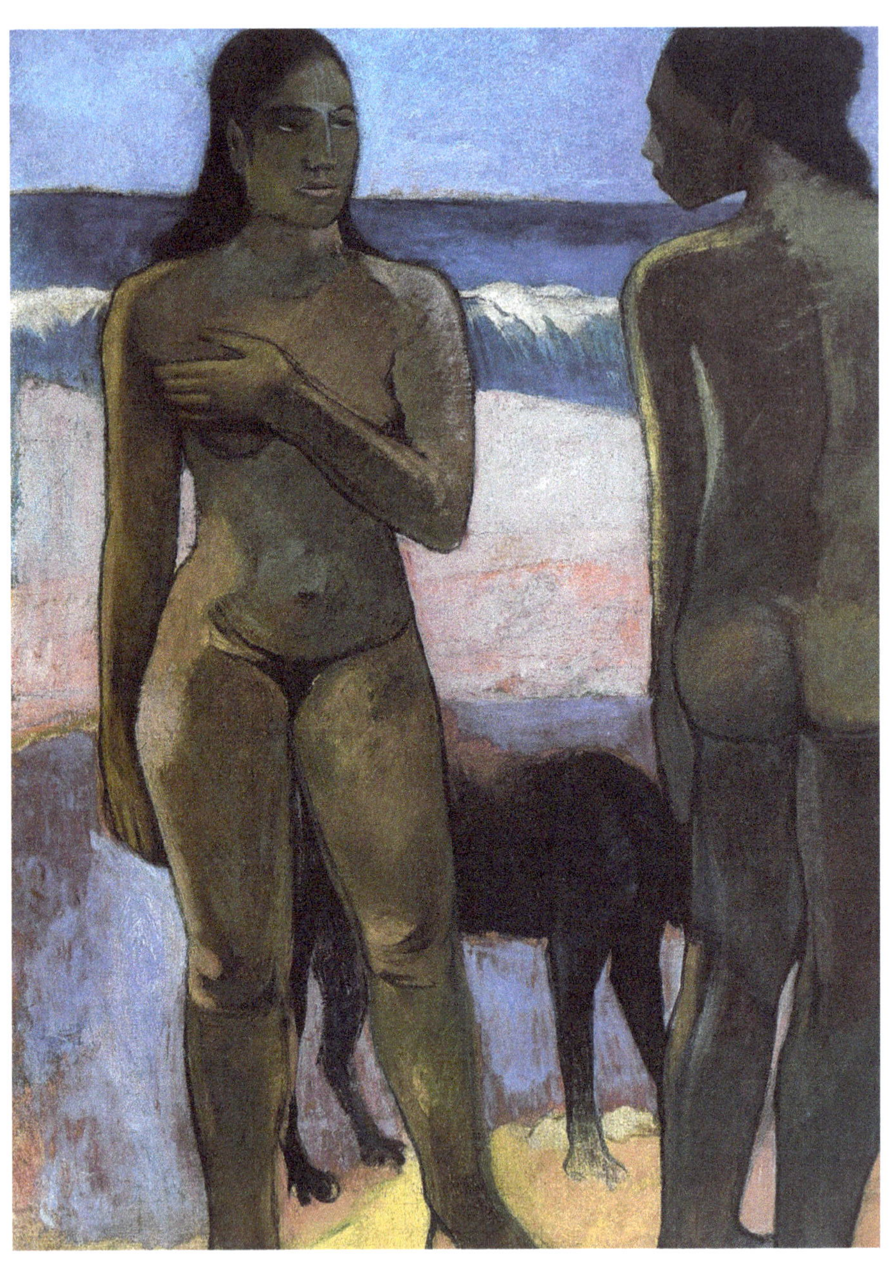

Paul Gauguin, *Two Nudes on a Tahitian Beach*, 1892

Paul Gauguin's
Two Nudes on a Tahitian Beach

"Be loving and you will be happy" —
the motto Gauguin carved on one of his frames
perhaps declaims his life's several loves:

his Danish wife and the five kids,
the woman who was his Tahitian lover,
and then there was Anna the Javanese,

the provocative mistress
he paraded down the streets of Paris
to *épater le bourgeois*.

Two Nudes on a Tahitian Beach,
a painting he started in Tahiti
and finished in Paris,

tries to have it more than one way,
a Tahitian beauty on the left
and Anna on the right.

Gauguin loved with abandon,
but abandon
is a two-edged word.

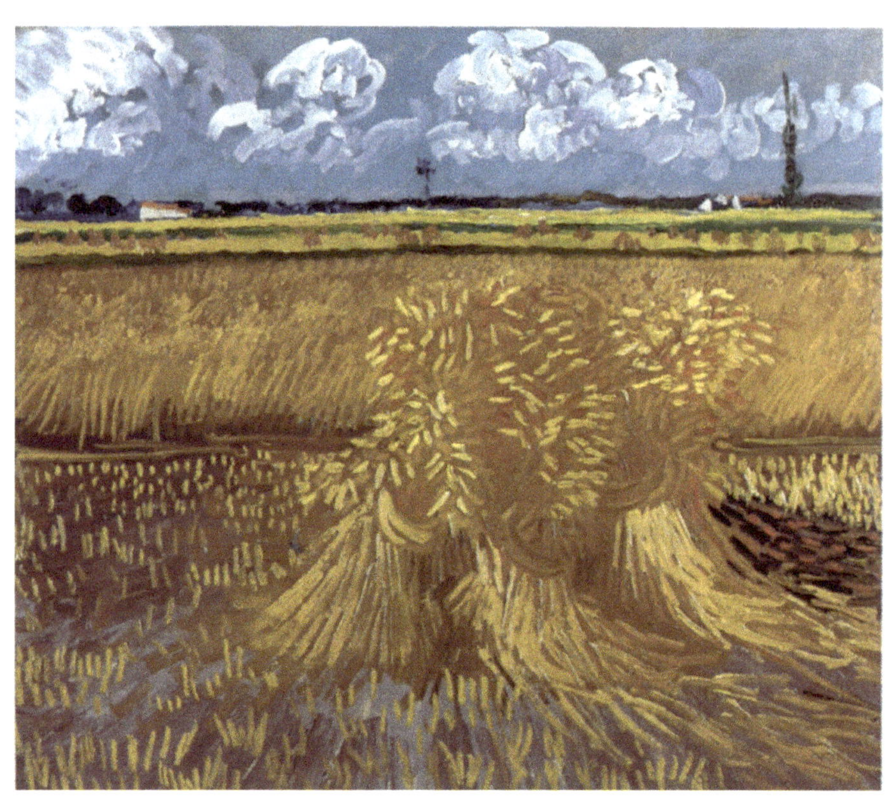

Vincent van Gogh, *Wheat Field*, 1888

Vincent Van Gogh's *Wheat Field*

Horizontal rows unfurl
a flag of Vincent's disposition,
line by line parallels
that make our eyes climb
one rung at a time:

first the new mown field
that foregrounds stubbled gold,
interwoven with violet accents,
stroke after stroke,
pulsating complementaries;

next the stern gleam
of the un-mown middleground stalks,
their yellow light gleaming between
thin lines of intervening green;

(continued)

then there aches the dark, distant boundary of trees
broken by a scattering
of red-roofed white dwellings
too far gone to dwell in.

At last
our eyes rise to meet the sky,
its worn wall of cool blue,
swirled with fierce musings of white cloud

that keep trying
to shout down
the too many shiny coins
of this seeing's dream.

Though there seems to be
no one at home here —
no Arlesian, Parisian, or Dutch
alive within this scene —

at the heart of all this
we arrive at the center ring,
the hard-to-see dance
of the several sheaves,
Vincent's complex presence

vividly invisible,
his gesturing's
manic choreography
adeptly lost in the gilded leaves
of his surrounding grief.

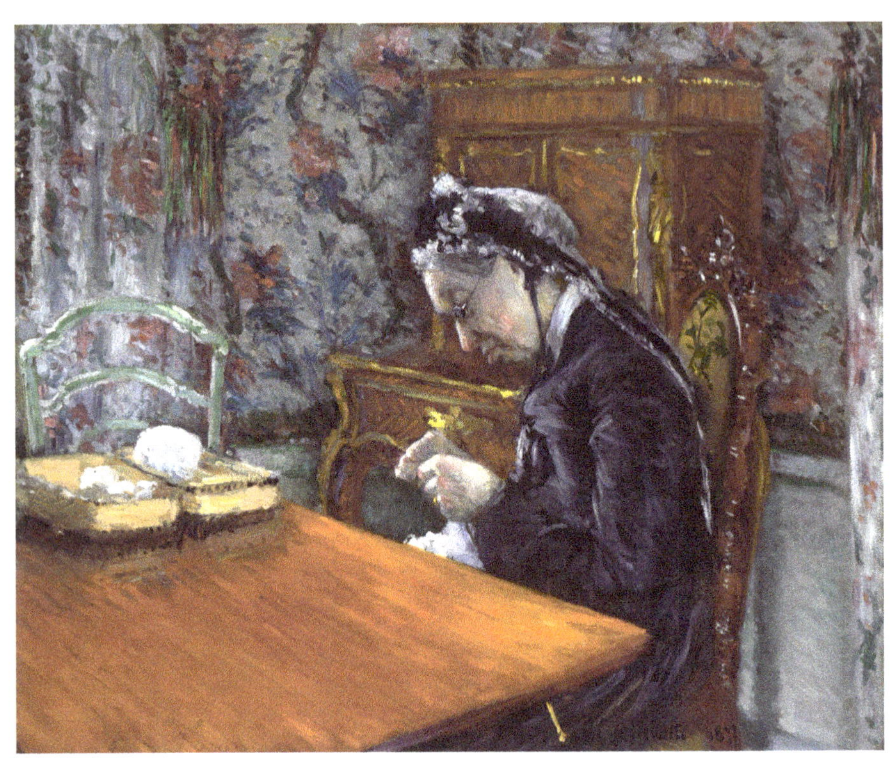

Gustave Caillebotte, *Mademoiselle Boissière Knitting*, 1877

Gustave Caillebotte's *Madame Boissière Knitting*

Madame Boissière is knitting a shawl
at the behest of Gustave Caillebotte,
the most genial of millionaires,
who has designed this trifle as a gift

for Charlotte, the mistress who will outlive
him by 30 years. Caillebotte records
with joy the precision of the seamstress,
in her plain black *haute bourgeoisie* attire,

who leans soberly and homely of face
into the bright, *impressionniste* light
of the window, whose draperies,
resplendent with floral designs,

seem entirely to contradict this plain
worker in thread Caillebotte shows
to be holding her own against
the *décoratif* decline of the day.

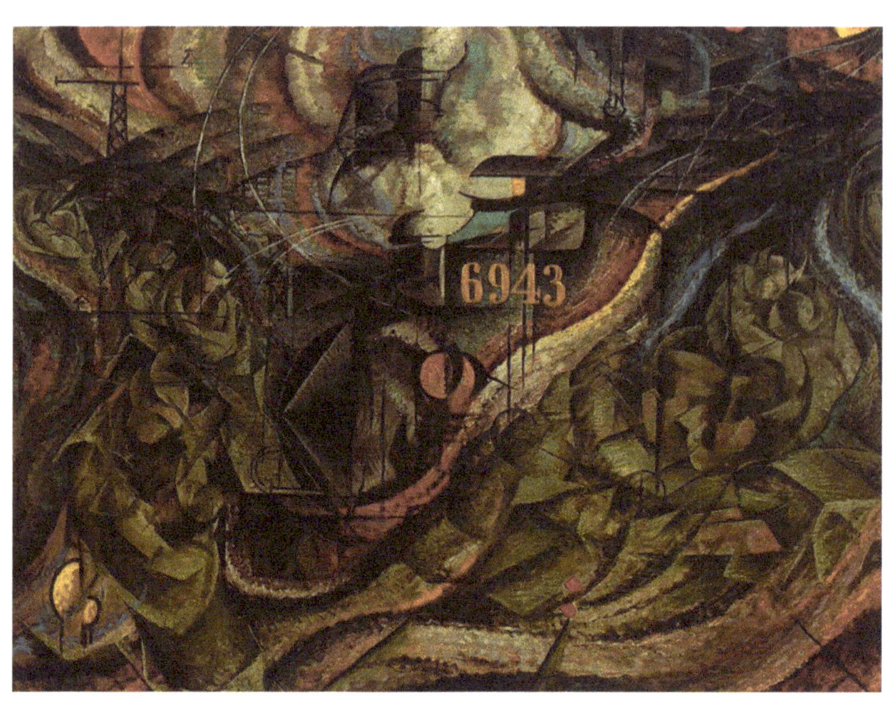

Umberto Boccioni, *States of Mind I: The Farewells*, 1911

Umberto Boccioni's *The Farewells*

We stand together, as if for the last time —
green always green our embracings,
though edged by twisted
risky misgivings of red and white.

Or are they risky missed givings?
Where joys and sorrows intervene
and intertwine as today,
yesterday, tomorrow, never?

We want to be, we imagine,
new and old and never ending
during our momentary stand together
on this platform of right now —

with the painted engine hissing
and swirls of Boccioni smoke obscuring
the forever of what we think we know,
as we stare at this canvas

and try to grasp the painted emptiness
that might, after all, be us.

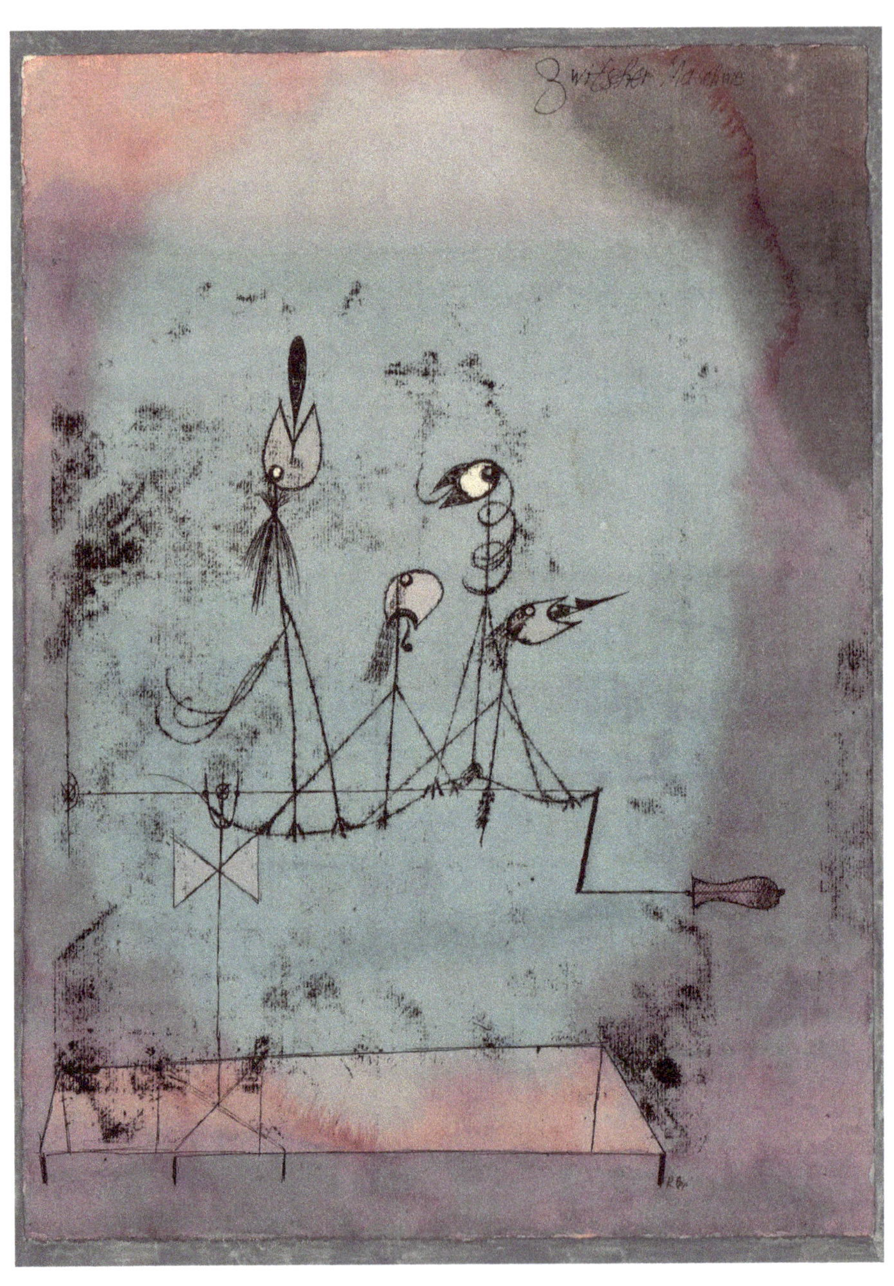

Paul Klee, *Twittering Machine*, 1922

Paul Klee's
Twittering Machine

A machine made of birds
composes a music,
each bird
a figure on the scale,

a note of the song,
twittering
with open beak
and exclamation point tongue

played by the turning
of the machine's crank.
It's as if a sweetly cruel device
compelled

the tree of the world
to love the sky
or, at the least,
to sing its tune.

René Magritte's *The Unexpected Answer*

The way out or the way in
might be a jagged hole
that breaks through

where you need to go,
despite the door
you might simply have opened.

Your advance cracks
a passage unexpected into
a darkness grim and oddly inviting.

The floorboards carry you forward
as if yours were an ordinary life,
while the absence of light

in the place that waits
would seem to be horrific
and comic all at once,

like the life-and-death
exits of Bugs Bunny
and Road Runner that rely

on impossibilities
through which no nemesis
could pass.

René Magritte's
When Evening Falls

When evening falls it should not break,
but might if night is all we know of day,
and nothing seems to be at stake.

If the horizon holds an ocean or a lake,
we think a boat could carry us away.
When evening falls it should not break.

We sought a night where we could undertake
an ending that would leave a word to say,
but nothing seems to be at stake.

Night, at least, should be without mistake,
but how get past the sorrow, the dismay?
When evening falls it should not break.

That distant castle could be for our sake,
an answer to the problems of the day,
but nothing seems to be at stake.

René Magritte's
Infinite Reconnaissance

A walk with a friend into the endless sky can be instructive,
especially when it's undertaken a few years before one's death,
especially when that friend is just another version of oneself.

Magritte enjoyed profoundly the pointlessness
   that is point of everything,
but it is hard to believe that absurdity
is all that horizon has to offer.

He needed to explain the silliness
of it all to himself over and over again,
as he does here in full —

Magritte brandishing his finger of index
to explain to Magritte
what they both understood to be

incomprehensible
but not all that
complex.

Seeing Things, American Wing

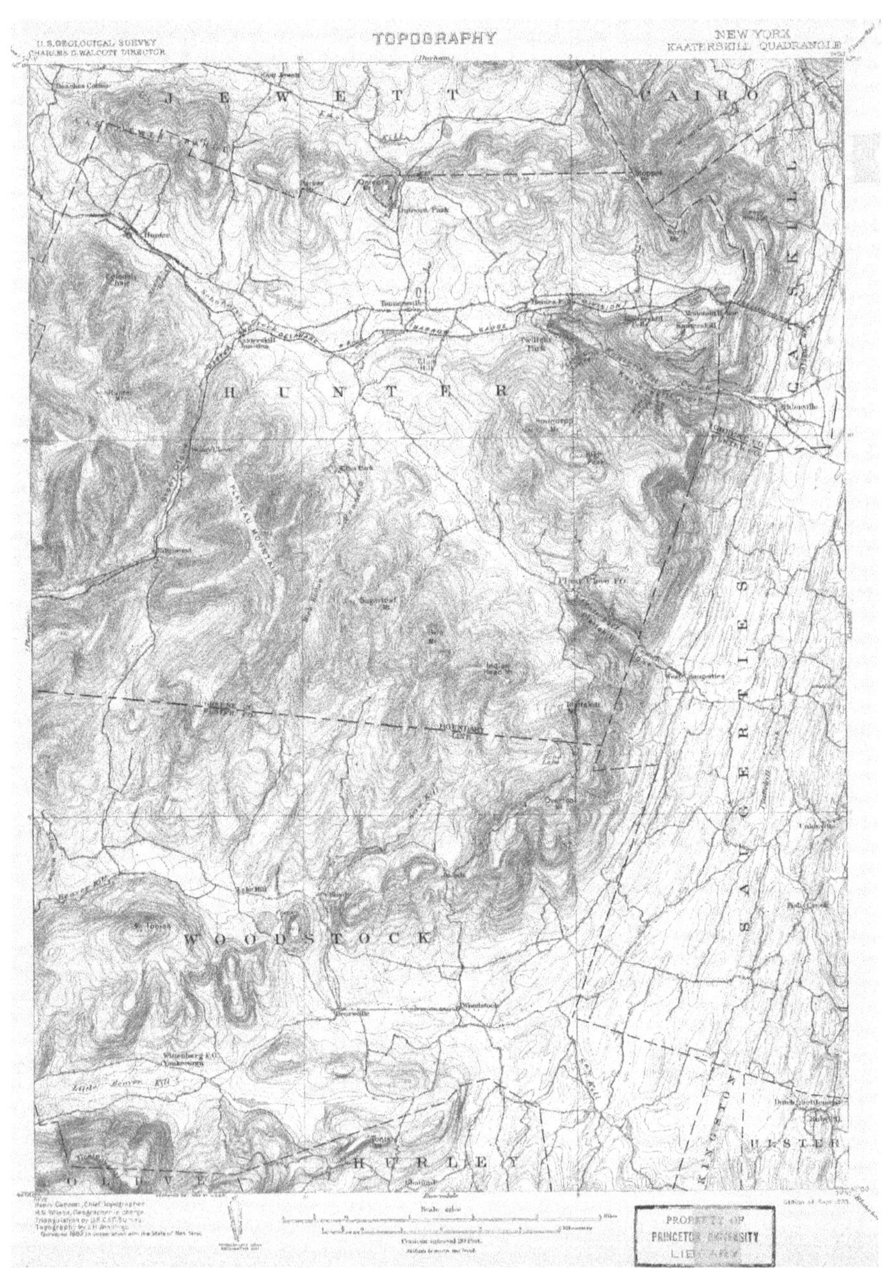

United States Geological Survey,
New York: Kaaterskill Quadrangle, 1903

United States Geological Survey Map, *Kaaterskill Quadrangle*

The swirl of flat lines seems
one of Pollack's abstract expressions —

no soaring mountains,
no plunging gorges,

only a thumbnail design,
a fingerprint of sorts,

left at the scene
by the guilty party:

God of course.

Thomas Cole's
Notch of the White Mountains

Cole knew the story, as did Emerson,
of the family that famously died here
in the sudden terror of avalanche,
caught in the narrowed notch.
as boulders tumbled down.

Strangely, the Willey's had
shifted shelter the day before
when a smaller avalanche threatened.
Placed in the path of the larger disaster
not all their bodies were ever found.

It was here, biographers say,
that Emerson decided to be Emerson,
abandoning a merely clerical career.
There is something —
for both Emerson and for Cole —

about the way this place brings
mountain against mountain,
about how intimately seen mighty things
can be picturesque and terrible, too,
that spoke to these devotees of a Nature

red with birch and oak,
an autumnal grandeur,
poetically almost apocalyptical,
a something brutal
they could sing.

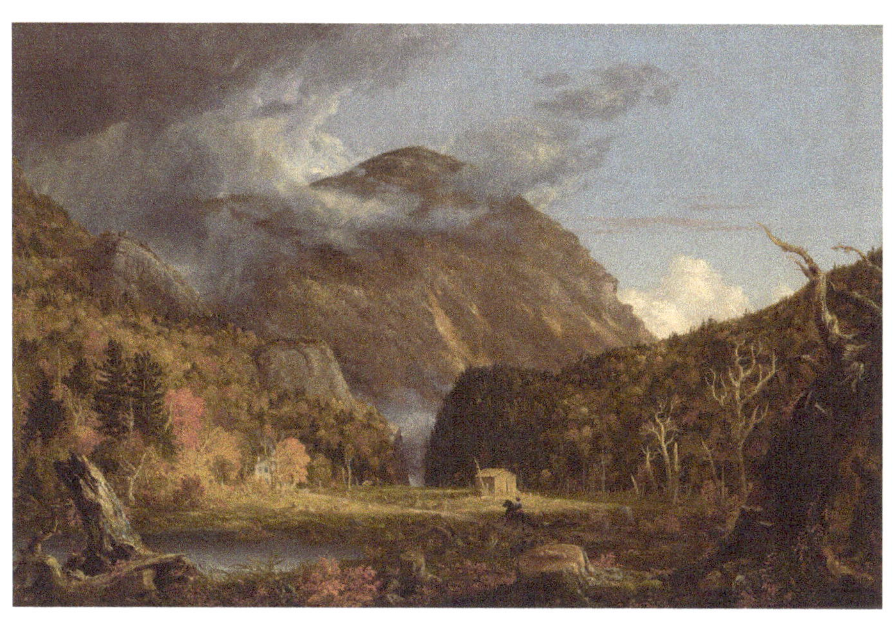

Thomas Cole, *A View of the Mountain Pass Called the Notch of the White Mountains (Crawford Notch)*, 1839

Thomas Cole's
The Voyage of Life

1. Childhood

The boat erupts from a cavern
under a mountain, shadowy,
craggy, and precipitous.
A wound gaping and unhealed
gives forth its child.
Out of the pained narrows
a luxuriance bursts
as way too many flowers,
even Egyptian blue lotus —
impossibly, a joy.

2. Youth

The stream almost seems
to steer into
the sky's cloud castle,
its hope's palest dome,
opalescent with possession,
as if nothing could be easier.

(continued)

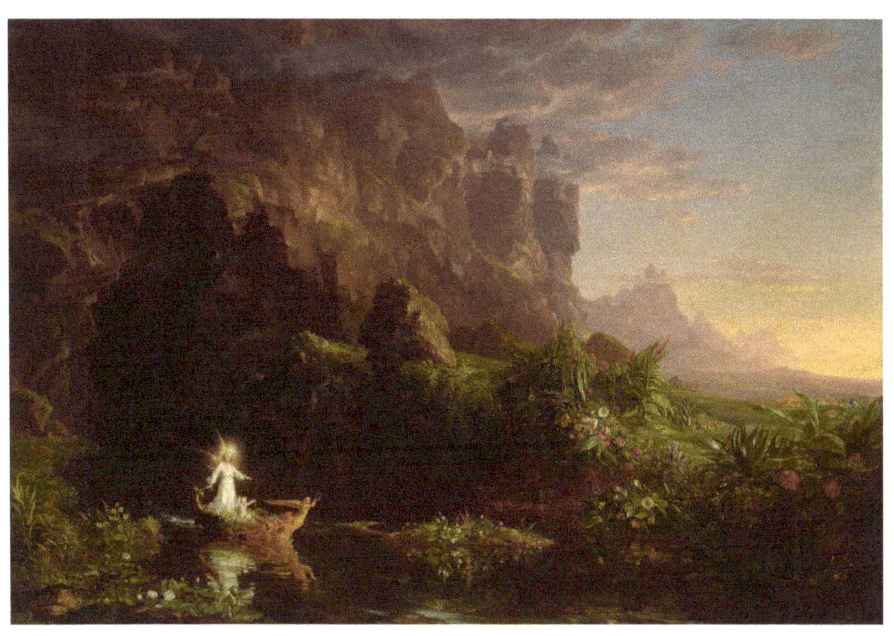

Thomas Cole, *The Voyage of Life: Childhood*, 1842

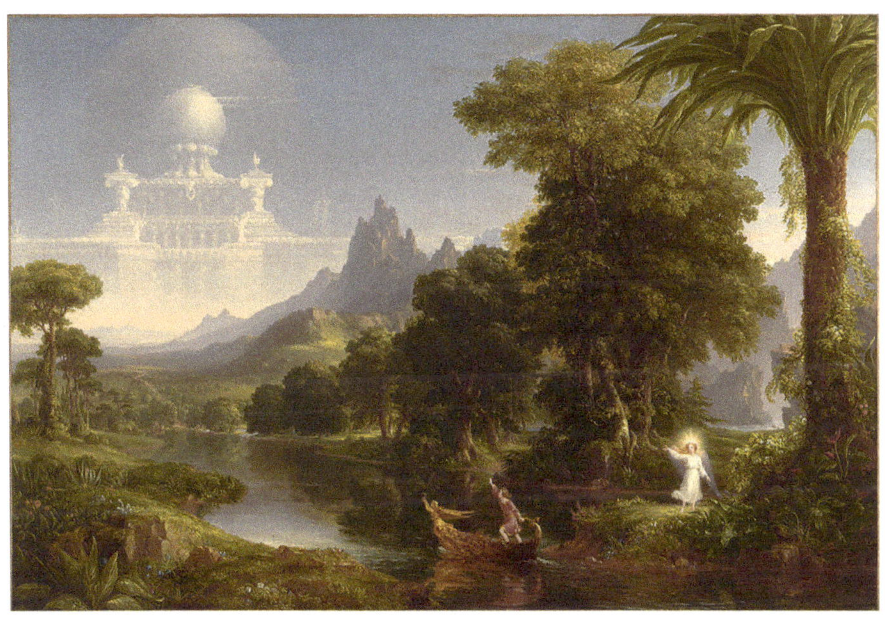

Thomas Cole, *The Voyage of Life: Youth*, 1840

3. Manhood

The voyager's adulterations
impel a swelling turbulence
and a plunging down
into a cataract
we should have known was coming.
In this unforgiving sky
demons lounge and glower
in lurid light.

4. Old Age

But now, suddenly,
the previously unseen forgiveness
is everywhere apparent —
as a relay race of angels,
their fragments of light,
afloat amidst the ridiculous dark
and the infinite expanse
of ocean, ocean, ocean.

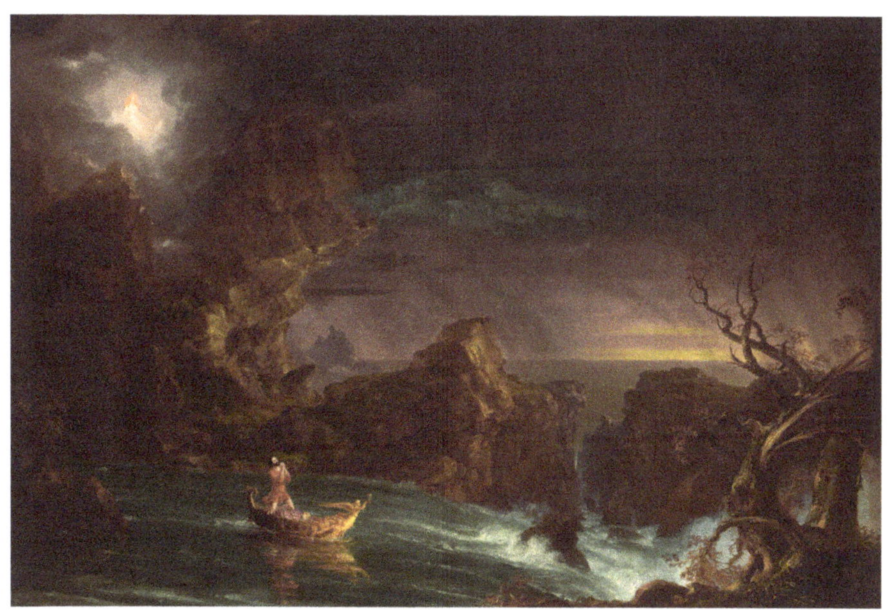

Thomas Cole, *The Voyage of Life: Manhood*, 1842

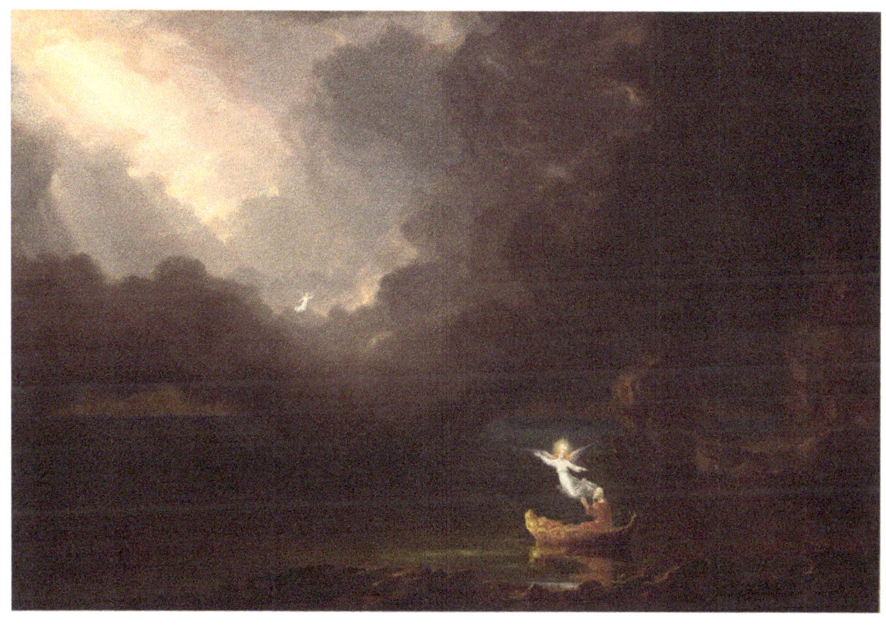

Thomas Cole, *The Voyage of Life: Old Age*, 1842

Pond at Cedarmere

This is where, in later years,
Bryant saw his waterfowl up close,
screaming among his fellows.

William Cullen — our first suburban poet,
the first of many to love Nature
because it was not New York City —

saw the flight of a Canada goose
as a sign that the divine
cruise control had us all in its sights.

Because that faith is hard to come by,
I pick up any stone as evidence
that the universe is cold

and gray and directionless
and fling it out over the waters,
watching its flat side skip three times

across the surface before sinking
beneath an indignant black beak
that rises, screaming now at me,

as if to say, by the magnificent
beating of wide wings, that he knows,
perfectly well, where he is going.

Storm at Cedarmere

for William Cullen Bryant

The sound swells and turns above Bryant's
autumnal home as rising winds flail
the trees, and pale-white mists shroud
upland steeps, turning gloom inside out,

hollowing clouds of bright such as Tom Cole
could color at the heights of Kaaterskill.
One bay window finds Bryant's pond a cold
bright stone of light in hands held out,

an offering to the slanting dark of rains
that won't end soon. The other window sees
the harbor wanting to keep on gleaming
beyond all drumbeat melancholias,

over full with remaining alive,
giving Bryant delicate redeemings —
sweet, dangerous dreams of almost seaward —
held to his long island's vastness of Sound.

Waking in the Catskills

There is no better place for dawn.
Here the cool and dark is a tender glove.
I can see why Winkle woke an elder man
after snoring for two decades above his clove.

I wake here at sunrise to watch the fog grow
then burn off the narrow lake that unfolds as dream,
an eight-mile lake whispering "water is all we know."
Floating birds, drifting clouds, and swaying trees seem

to agree, wanting, I suppose, to go with that flow.
When I pull open the drapes this morning,
a large sandhill crane, head cocked to the gentle glow,
is walking along the dock directly towards me.

Though he is a rarer bird here than me,
he is the one who squawks when our eyes meet.

Frederic Edwin Church's *Andes of the Ecuador*

A landscape can be a universe,
a kosmos Church thought,
as big and as tiny as South America

that comes down to the last leaf,
comes down to the tiniest bird,
comes up with the soul.

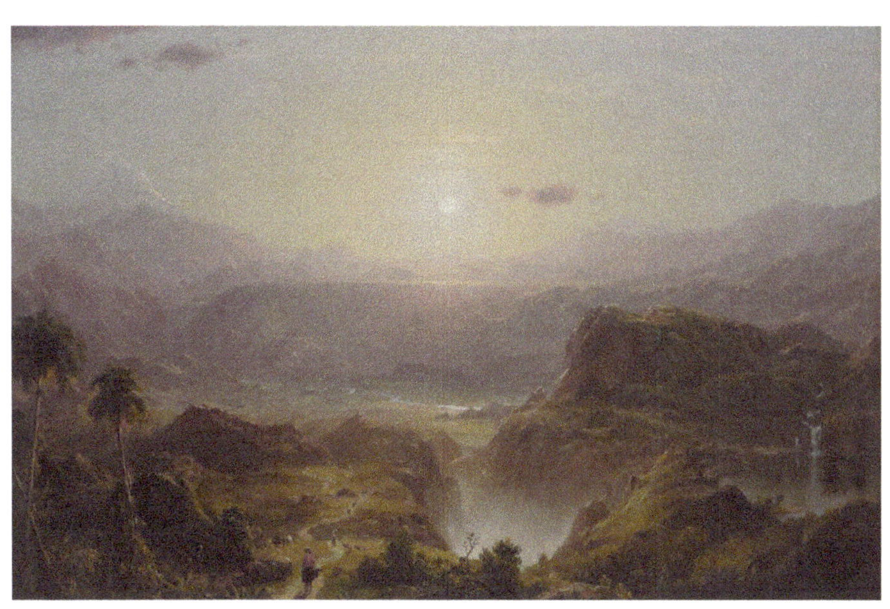

Frederic Edwin Church, *Andes of the Ecuador*, 1855

Raphaelle Peale's *Still Life with Oranges*

Raphaelle's short life was stilled
by taxidermy chemicals or alcoholism or epilepsy
or all of the above,

but still he had a life in art, an art in life
arranged as things gathered
and held still,

nature morte
so that the paintings might live —
the fruit of his labors here

mostly a basket case,
except for that one orange
outside the weave,

foreground center,
that signifies the artist
by means of its unpeeling.

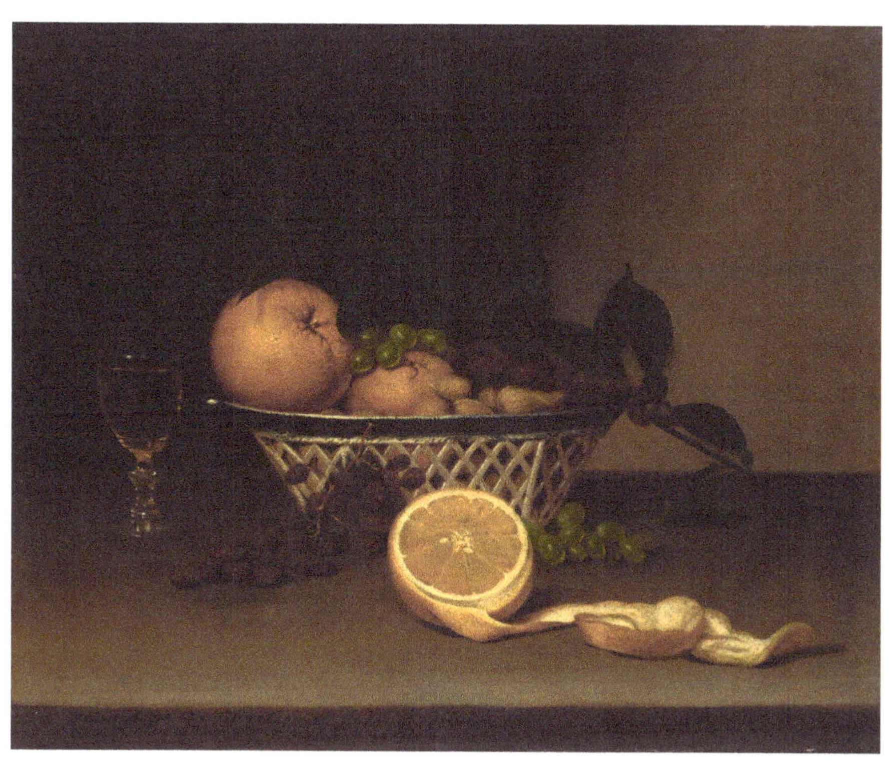

Raphaelle Peale, *Still Life with Oranges*, 1818

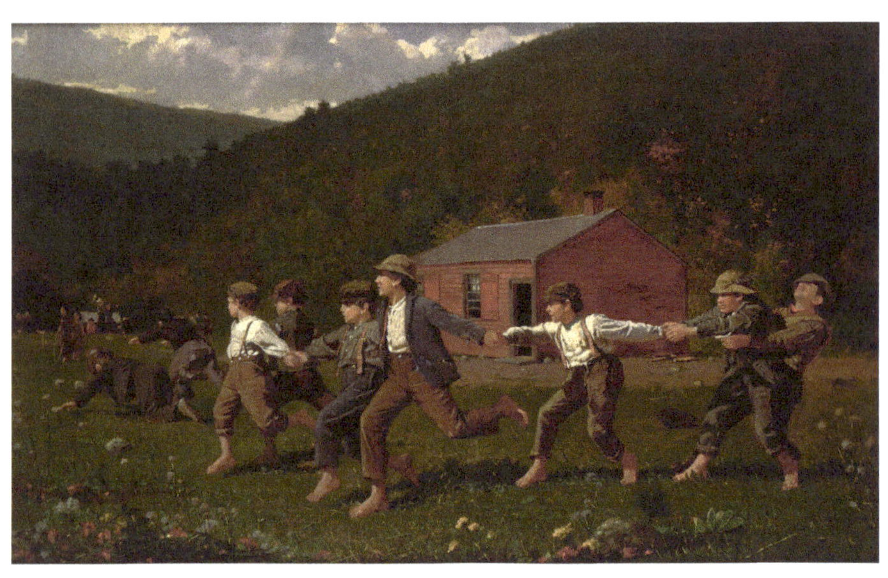

Winslow Homer, *Snap the Whip*, 1872

Winslow Homer's *Snap the Whip*

Snap the whip is a game of run and fall,
of wanting to hang on but falling after all.
The running takes the boys towards
a goal that must be nothing in particular —

an open meadow, an expanse of flowers,
a distant mountain, a waiting schoolhouse.
The point of the game is holding on —
deftly, desperately —

but there would seem to be,
at last, no way to win, no way to lose.
The yank-back team is composed
of all who have fallen so far;

therefore this game, if not for weariness
or the end of recess,
could go on refining its fall and rise
until the end of time.

Winslow Homer's *Moonlight*

A man and a woman reclining on a beach
facing a declining of the moon into the sea
could be a dream,
even a dream come true,

if they are lovers or in line to be,
but here we have the imbalance
of affection that most of us
have known or imagined or both.

This man adores this woman.
That much is clear.
The inclination of his figure
displays the inclination of his mind.

His face, too, is facing hers.
She eclipses for him,
it would seem,
this most resplendent moon.

But the woman tends the other way,
looking to the horizon for things to say.
Her open fan, unnecessary in the cool of night,
seems poised to fend this fellow off.

When Winslow painted this picture
he was in full retreat in the Hamptons,
while Helena was off in the Big City
marrying her Gilder.

In this picture's frame,
Winslow keeps her in mind
for his fond fantasy's sake

(though she is entirely,
he is emphatically telling himself,
out of reach)

This one last water-colored Helena moment,
knows that moons must set
and waves on beaches break.

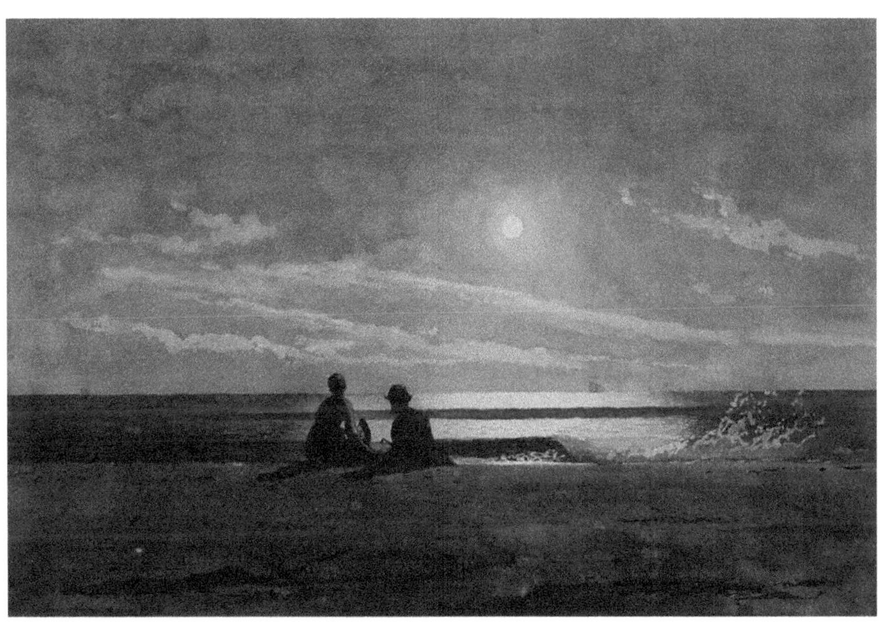

Winslow Homer, *Moonlight*, 1874

Winslow Homer's *Sunset Fires*

The dysfunctions of art
(those who want it do not want to pay for it)
underscore the dysfunctions of love
(a man without income cannot marry).

To be alone might be best, Homer decided,
so in 1880 he lived in a lighthouse at Gloucester —
a lighthouse is ideal for isolation
with water on three sides.

Water can be, he would always remember,
a buffer against all that's broken in heart or mind,
but water, too, with color added,
had become for him a means to catch the world,

even at end of day
when everything from sea to sky,
from horizon to shore,
seemed to be on fire.

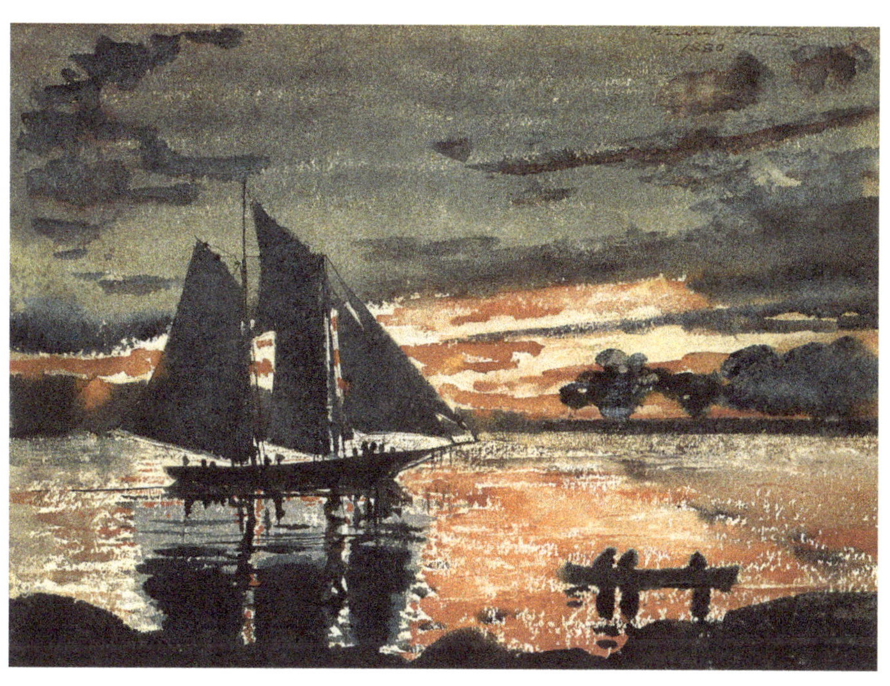

Winslow Homer, *Sunset Fires*, 1880

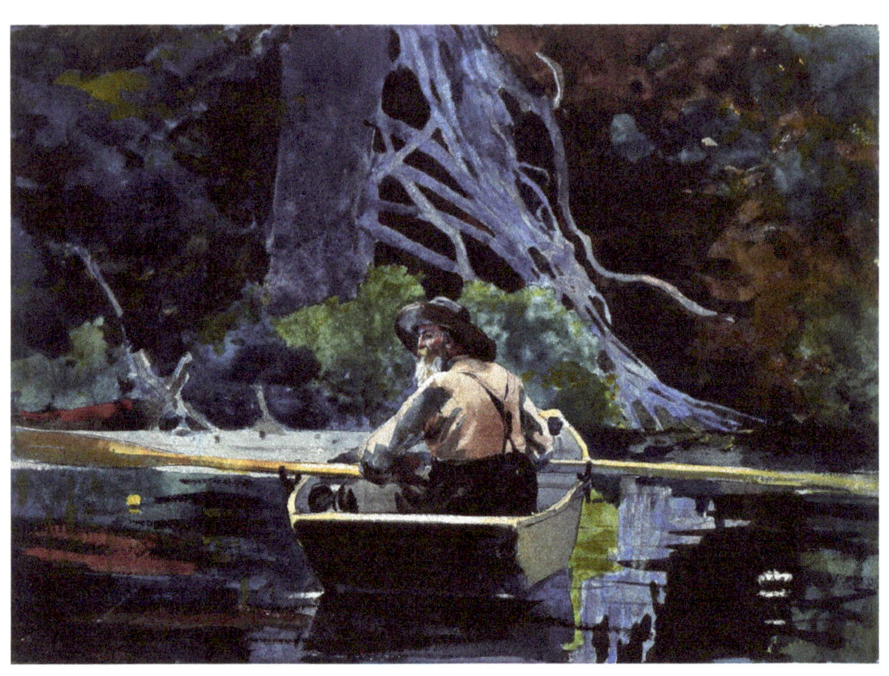

Winslow Homer, *The Adirondack Guide*, 1894

Winslow Homer's *The Adirondack Guide*

Paper can take on water
for the sake of color.
In this watercolor the theme
might be, at bottom, water.

At top Homer floats
an Adirondack guide
crossing an Adirondack scene,
oars raised above a pond
that reflects a delicate sheen
of black, brown, blue, and green.

We could say, too, that Homer
reflects on what it is
to be an old guy, wry and wiry,
isolate and emphatic of expression,
capped by a broken brown hat,
suspended in thought as well as on paper —

turning to us a sharp-nosed, bearded profile —
as if to say he knows damn well
what this moment
does not need to mean.

Winslow Homer's *An October Day*

A day in October can be lovely —
autumnal trees, rising as flaming verticals
against the green slopes of Beaver Mountain
and descending down the paper,
as reflections in
the bright blue of Mink Pond,

but, against this song of October glamor,
witness the hounding in its midst:
the hunter rowing the blue boat
towards a desperately swimming buck.

The buck fears the barking
of the determined dog on the far bank.
The hunter and the deer both know
the dog will not allow the deer
to come ashore alive.

As so often in Winslow's scenes,
we face a matter of life and death,
that insists upon a gorgeous world,
while never forgetting
there will be a meal in a hall
and a head on a wall.

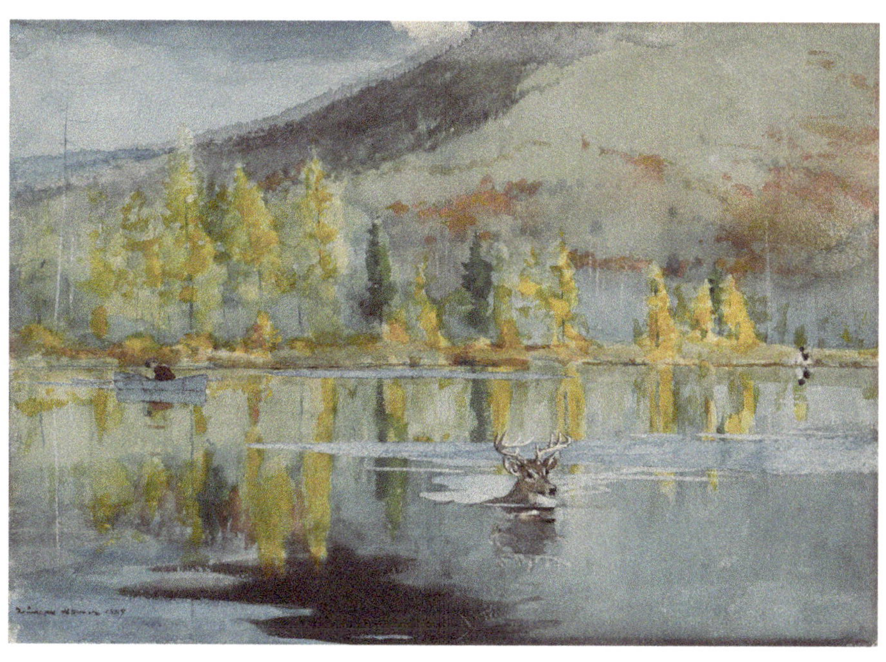

Winslow Homer, *An October Day*, 1889

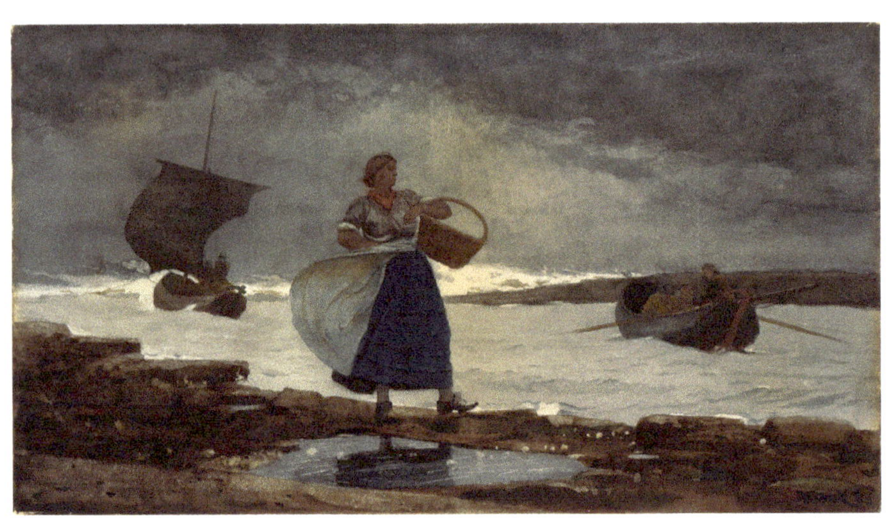

Winslow Homer, *Inside the Bar*, 1883

Winslow Homer's *Inside the Bar*

At Cullercoats,
Homer saw women
as extraordinary.
A fishwife stands alone here,
staunch and steady
on a wave-rocked reef.

Her apron billows in high wind,
but she balances against it,
one arm akimbo,
the other holding the basket
the fishermen
will overfill with fish,
their coble approaches from the rear.

Though this occasion
could not be more ordinary,
Homer shows this woman to be
a presence gigantic,
her monumentality
connecting rocky shore and sky
and the sea that comes between.

Winslow Homer's *Sunlight on the Coast*

There is sunlight, we note, on the coast.

We see the sun declare its need to set
on the horizon just off Prout's Neck.
Its gleam breaks through clouds
as a swatch of bright where sea touches sky.

Light here tumbles on crests, foams in backwash,
flickers on slick edges of black rock,
and glows translucent blue
in a wave's gathering roll.

Homer knows that his painted light
is headed towards oceanic dark,
but he loves that its last moments
are everywhere apparent

a withdrawal from one world
in behalf of the next
on a coast where light is endlessly broken,
ceaselessly repaired.

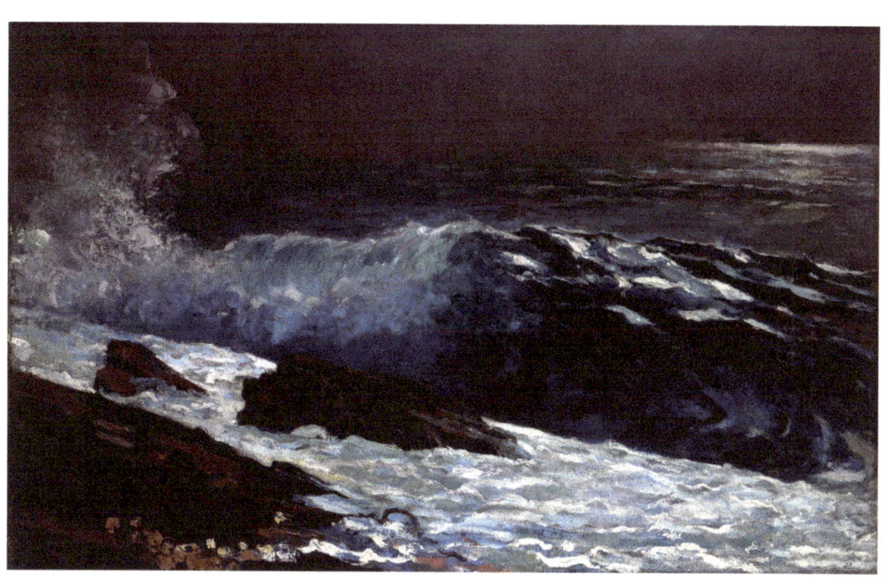

Winslow Homer, *Sunlight on the Coast*, 1890

Joseph Stella's *Brooklyn Bridge*

In his first painting of it,
lines of force slant this way, then slant that,
flickering a cacophony of blue and white
above a blossom of blood;
while the spine articulates —
in tiny, elegant detail —
the sequenced towers.

Passing this *frisson futurisme*
in subsequent pictures,
Stella settled to a symmetry
a quintessential *modernisme*
that became the way he crossed
this bridge every subsequent time
he came to its soaring contradictions —

medieval gothic are its massive piers
and yet the machined-aged cables of steel,
the taut song of its wiring *mechanique*,
is what lifts our spirits, transports us,
as we walk the interior passage,
unique to this suspension,
a path that makes our walking seem

a transit towards an altar,
an altar that turns out to be
the City of Brooklyn,
a place worthy of worship in its way,
but cruel, ungraspable.
"Only the dead know Brooklyn,"
sayeth the gospel of Thomas Wolfe.

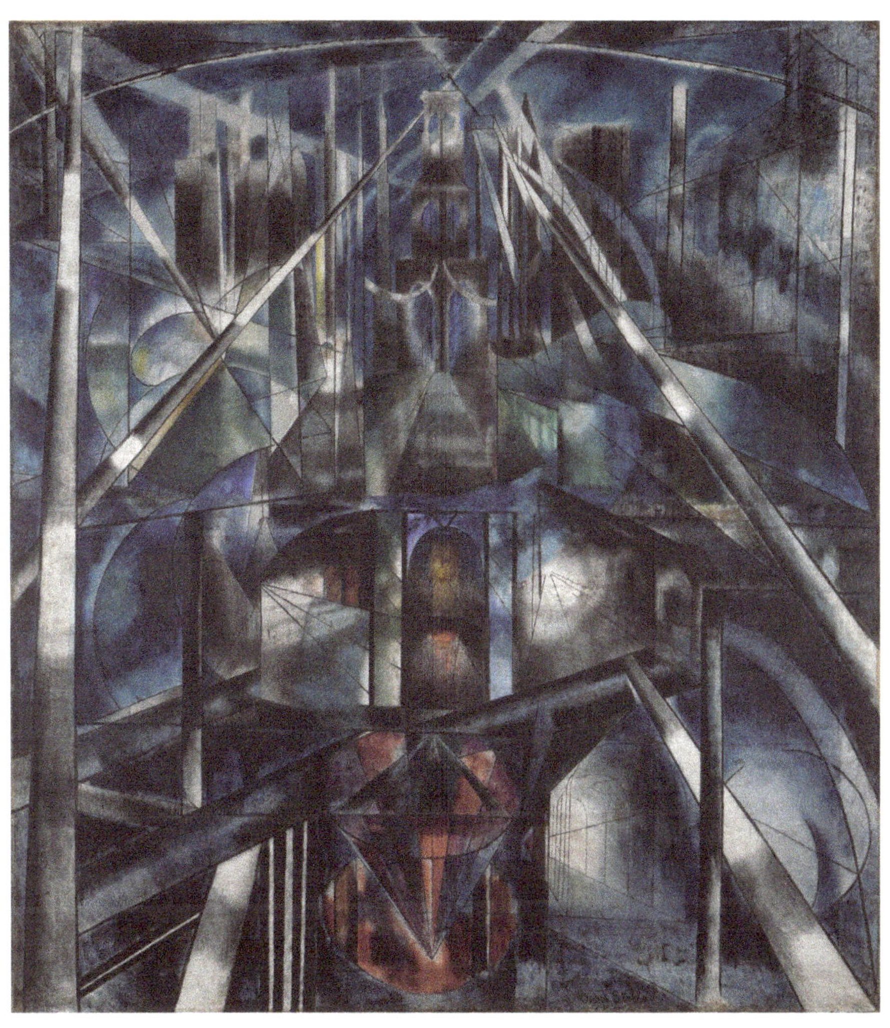

Joseph Stella, *Brooklyn Bridge*, 1919–20

Edward Hopper's Color Notes for *Route 6, Eastham*

After Hopper designed a scene,
he'd plan his colors.

His notes for this picture place
"pale green" on one wall,
"pale warm grey" on another,
"pale lavender" on still another.

His shadows tumble in one direction
as "dark warm lavender,"
and as "cold shadow" in the other.
All he wanted , he once said,
was to paint sunlight
on the side of a building.

Here we see him making light
one color at a time.

Edward Hopper's *Freight Cars, Gloucester*

The foreground grass flickers bright in gold and green.
The burgundy freight cars remain on track;
they are the mid-ground stars of Hopper's scene.
Married four years now, Eddie and Jo are back
again painting in their honeymoon spot.
At right angles to the trains and Gloucester roofs
a sun-smacked pole holds up the picture's top.

Jo's figure remains unseen in this view —
she's down by the harbor painting the boats
with her old pals — artistes of nothing new,
they're, like Jo, not destined to be of note.
Yet Jo's on Eddie's mind. His strokes of fire,
the foreground grasses strike and strike again,
suggest, at bottom, he's not without desire.

Edward Hopper's *The City*

A corner of a square is a view
to look down upon in 1927:

this clash of architectures startles,
a striking cacophony

centered on a monstrously lovely Victorian verticality,
its decoratively mansarded façade

up rising through the picture's heart.

Edward Hopper's *Room in New York*

Seated in the room's one comfortable chair
a husband hunches forward, intent upon his paper
as if his life depended on the scores he finds there.

Just home from work
he has not yet loosened his tie,
nor spoken with his wife

who is wearing her bright red dress,
the one with the bow in back that
comes easily undone.

She knows he has not noticed
so she plunks the keys of her piano
to say to him softly

that she is there
and has been waiting all day
for him.

The room glows —
yellow walls, oak table and door,
the rosy tones of the man's chair and the woman's dress.

Something could come of this.

Edward Hopper's *Summer Evening*

On the porch of Hopper's childhood home
in Nyack on the Hudson
a memory shapes a picture.

His sister, Marion,
who will never marry,
listens to a young man tell her something —

what he is saying does not make her happy.
Nothing explains her dismay or how this scene
turned the rest of her life against her

and away from the earnest blond man;
turned her into the spinster sister
of a famous painter.

Edward Hopper's *Stairway*

This stairway
takes us down
to a doorway
open far too wide
to a brooding mass
of shadowy trees —

one of Hopper's
favorite jokes:
a path
we cannot help
but take
that leads
only
to dark.

Edward Hopper's *Haunted House*

A haunted house, an emptied shell,
stands against a gray day in 1926.
Broken windows, a scattering of holes,
hint the house is beyond what tools can fix.

Hopper paints the shadows of the dormers
as gorgeous rows of purpled blues,
revealing how light can render
unexpected felicities of hue

and inexplicable solidities of shape.
Meanwhile subtle inflections of darkness
reach long limbs down a sloping grade,
shadow arms that hint of a grasping ghost.

A little joke Hopper whispers;
his house haunted by his laughter.

Edward Hopper's *House of the Foghorn*

Critics wondered why Hopper
so often painted
this nondescript

little white box of brick,
whose only distinction seemed to be
its tall red chimney.

Hopper admired its shapes
and its shadows, of course,
but the other reason was simply

that he and Jo were so often there —
eating, as they loved to do,
at the clam shack next door.

Edward Hopper's *On the Quai: The Suicide*

It's the one time Hopper
shows us the horrific,
but, even in this instance,
in which a man is about to die,
broken and bloody on the stones
of the Quai,

forty-five feet below the bridge
he is about to leap from,
what Hopper gives us is
nothing more than the calm
of the suicide's despair,
isolate

above the railing of the bridge
and beneath the shadows
of the tall buildings
that line the Seine embankment
and against the endless blank haze
of river and sky,

touched lightly with white and gray,
one vast expanse
across which the truncated bridge
can only extend its long arm
without hope of grasping
anything.

Edward Hopper's *Two Comedians*

Eddie was 83, sick and slowing
towards an ending when he painted
himself and Jo taking a last bow
on a stage *commedia dell'arte.*

In early sketches he is Harlequin,
the trickster dressed in diamond designs,
the guy who always wins
over death and all else.

and Jo alone is garbed in Pierrot white,
the uniform of the fool,
who, because of innocence and a kind heart,
always loses.

In the end, though,
Eddie painted himself
in white, too, accepting, it seems,
the inevitable sweetness of defeat,

but he retained his dark trickster hat,
as if he'd kept at least
one more trick up his,
presumably white, sleeve.

Edward Hopper's *A Woman in the Sun* and Giovanni Bellini's *Saint Francis in the Desert*

Bellini's Francis seems ecstatic, expectant,
arms spread wide to receive
a statement of divine light,
stigmata faintly visible on each palm.

Stand before the painting
in the lush living room of the Frick
and see how the Godly beam
hits a patch of leaves in the tree on the left
in its path towards
the face, frock, and hands of the waiting saint.

Note how this burst of bright
throws Francis's shadow behind him,
while in the background
a donkey, a heron, and a shepherd
stand shadowless.

Hopper's woman possesses, too,
a shadow to be reckoned with,
but she seems desolate and accidental,

(continued)

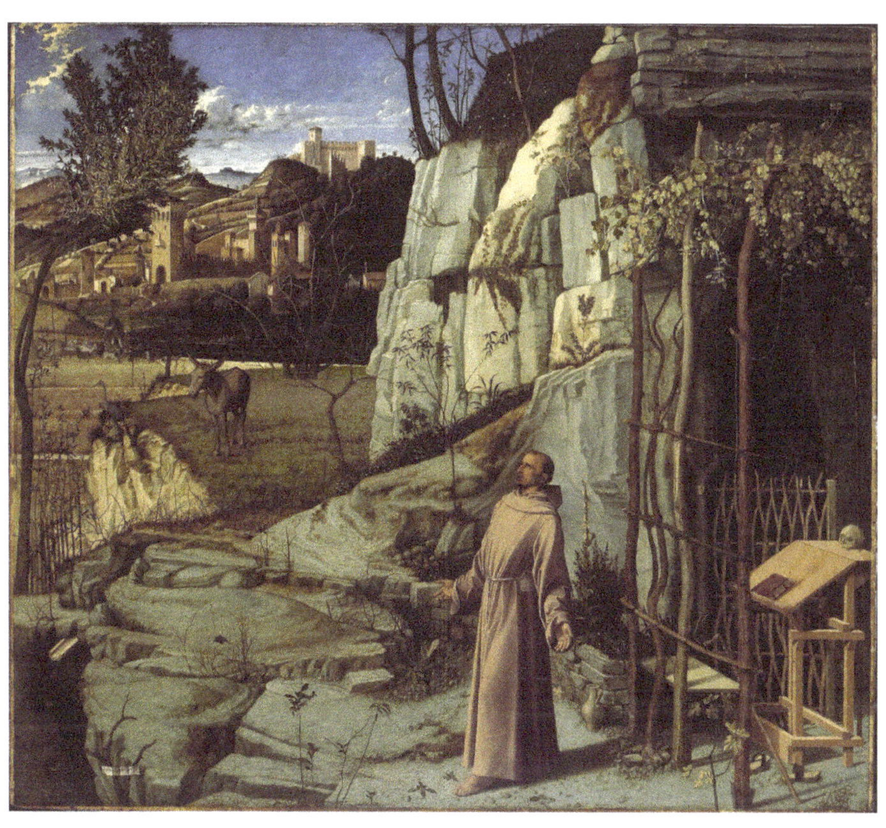

Giovanni Bellini, *Saint Francis in the Desert*, c. 1480

as she lingers in a streak of golden light
as if to ask a question
or receive an answer.
Hopper called her a "wise tramp."

See her up against the industrial white of the Whitney
sanctified by her desert-island morning
(we can glimpse two Cape Cod dunes through a window).
This sordid saint offers attributes —

the cigarette in her hand,
the high-heeled black shoes under her bed,
the complete nakedness of no clothes in sight —
but her sad sad face would seem to have found no God.

As I place the reproductions in front of me,
the Hopper on my left,
the Bellini on my right,
the two figures seem
to converse
but what they say

is only light.

Ansel Adams's *Moonrise, Hernandez, New Mexico*

A dot of moon over a smear of clouds,
a low horizon of snow-capped peaks
distantly glimpsed,
a foreground of adobe church

beside a village of small houses, and,
at the lowest edge of the cropped view,
an expanse of graveyard,
every white cross gleaming

as bright as the clouds,
as bright as the moon —
the moon whose craterous skull of a face
smiles grimly, in perfect focus,

seeming to claim its joke remains,
necessarily, beyond us.

Isamu Noguchi's Marble Loves

Noguchi loved marble and its elegant grains.
He loved the colors of the stones
and the colors of their names,
redolent of places, geology, and pigment:

arni, bardiglio, black austrian porticoi,
black marguinia, black petit-ganit,
carrara, yellow sienna,
persian travertine, italian, portuguese, greek,
green serpentine, pink serpentine, red alicante.

With epoxy he adhered them one to the other
in gorgeous austerely decorative displays
that speak to the example
of Brancusi's lovely classicisms.

His always deft titles sometimes spoke
to the voids of Sartre, the walkings of Giacometti,
and the suns and waterfalls of the wide world
he wanted art to comprehend,

but most of all his marbles evoke,
without naming names, the women he loved:
torso, woman, she, she number 2, elbow,
even his gateways are sexy, even his suns.

Most often the erotic is covert,
but in 1971
he went beautifully explicit
in *To Love (two elements)*.

Madame Groeda Weyrd Interprets You by Means of *The Fantod Pack*

for Edward Gorey

Écorché lays bare your plight —
your morbid sensibility,
the accident on the pier,
your confinement by irregularities.

The urn represents the sixties —
your busted heart, the forged invitation,
the mumbling sickness, the injustice,
the miscalculation.

The sea defines the outer world —
the mishap in January,
the lurching sickness, the chagrin,
the wasting, the secret enemy.

The insects bespeak your green ailments,
your senseless talk, your lost vitality,
the arrival of the disagreeable news,
the ambiguous threats in the cornfield.

The tunnel is your inner self —
the unpleasant discovery, the panic,
the angst, the boredom,
the remnant that might be who you are.

H. C. Westermann's *Nouveau Rat Trap*

"'It puzzles me, too,' he answered when asked the meaning of one of his sculptures."

He has built a better one
so we have beat a path
to the door of his trap,

a lovely assemblage of birch,
rosewood, metal, and rubber
that curves with an elegance

new and nouveau, too.
His joke as historical
as it is hysterical.

Yoko Ono's *A Hole to See the Sky Through*

I have long loved
this Yoko Ono card.

An artifact of 1971,
this lovely simplicity
of bright-white cardboard

I first held in my hands
in New York City in 1979.

I want to say it is very funny,
but there is no need to laugh.
Hold your eye to the hole   and look up.

And, yes, she is right!
The sky is right there!

Painting the Corners

Deryl Mackie's
Smokey Joe Williams

Dressed in the grays of one of his teams,
Smokey Joe — aka Cyclone Joe, aka the Texan Giant —
stands relaxed with ball in hand —
his calm in contrast
to the fury of his pitches —
faster than Satchell, faster than them all —
"the speed of a pebble in a storm"
commented one of his owners,
and then there were his changing speeds.
"If I throw them really hard,
they won't see them at all,"
he once commented, knowing, as he did,
that at least the umpire had to see the ball.

Famously in one game he fanned twenty-seven.
Ty Cobb claimed he would be
a "sure 30-game winner" in the white leagues.
One season he won 41 in the black leagues.
Almost always he won,
even when barnstorming white superstars.

In 1999, forty years after his death,
his plaque finally arrived in the Hall at Cooperstown.
But this portrait by Mackie,
which also resides in Cooperstown,
outshines the plaque in the Plaque Hall.

With bravura brushstrokes
Mackie renders in acrylic
the pose of the famous photo —
treating Williams' quiet demeanor
within a shimmer of Caribe clime —
Cuba probably —

rendered in fauve-like colors —
orange sky, violet palm trees, resplendent grass
(two kinds of greens interwoven with strokes
of blue, red, yellow, beige, and black).

It's a kind of justice really;
possibly the best pitcher ever to play the game —
so long ignored and once almost unknown —
residing now as the star of the Hall's collection.

Tim Swartz's *Stretching*

In this watercolor
the artist gives us elegance
of color and line,
discovered, no doubt, in a photo,
or in the veteran himself—

red-uniformed and red-haired—
stretching in spring-training green grass,
the strain of the stretch evidenced
only by his open mouth,
ever so slightly gasping for more air.

Dan Quisenberry, here at his great career's end,
playing now, surprisingly (ironically?)
for the St. Louis Cardinals,
is striving to extend his play one more year,
relying on near flawless control

of his low-velocity, submarine sinker.
He is stretching to be the best he could be,
despite his joking contention
that he was only a non-athlete's athlete,
that he had found a delivery in his flaw.

So sadly a cancer killed him
just a few years past this picture,
but, by that time, he had stretched again
to become a better and better baseball poet,
throwing lines that got past, or almost,

that dreaded cleanup hitter,
the one whose scythe whistles
the ninth-inning tune,
that terrible walk-off swing
that can knock even the best of us out of the box.

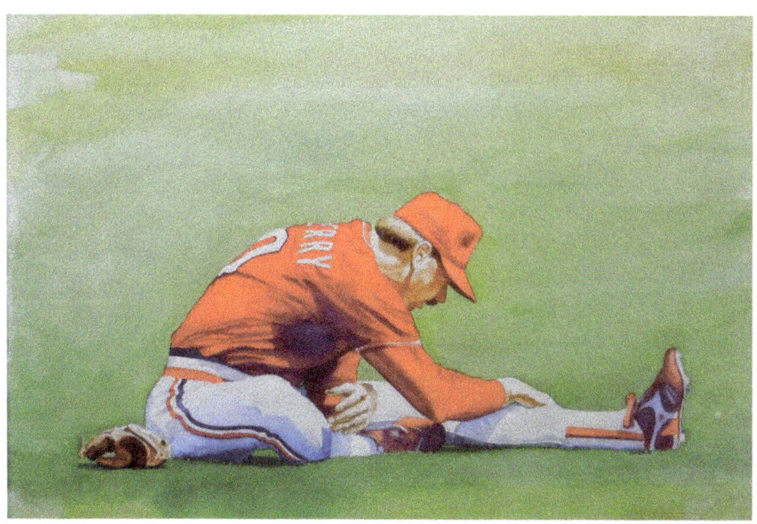

Tim Swartz, *Stretching II*, 1990

Ben Shahn's
Vacant Lot

Meticulously realistic,
this abstracted scene plays
with and against its world.

Certainly, the play of the boy
in the vacated lot
might mean that becoming a man

could be a standing against
thousands of bricks,
the compiled negativity

of the desperate wall that was 1939,
a hopelessness of desperation
and despair that Shahn

so often and so emphatically
painted and photographed.
Shahn felt in his bones

the passageway from the Depression
to World War that had to be,
for all of us,

a lonely, abandoned, degraded place.
And yet he also grasped,
courtesy of his haunted childhood,

that the boy he depicts in this vacancy
cannot be contained within
the terrors of his times.

As with all children, this boy,
a surrogate for the irrepressible Shahn,
emphatically possesses himself

and what he hopes his future will be
and swings away — passionately, precisely —
at whatever bounces his way.

Robert Riggs'
The Impossible Play

Master painter of circuses and fisticuffs,
Riggs celebrated what muscle and mass can try to do.
This painting is wide and narrow, impossibly so,
a work few walls could hold. Impossible, too,
is the vigor of its foreground figures,
incredibly massive
from the bottom of the picture to the top,
from the left edge to the right.

The expertly bunting batter
takes up half the width,
but there is also room —
because of the horizontal expanse —
for display of most of the umpire and all of the catcher.
In the sparkling background,
tiny dots give us a vast array of spectatorship,
a crowd depiction cramped and colossal.

The rest of the cast also excites the eye:
especially the middle distance figures —
the pitcher, the third baseman, the third-base coach,
and the runner, breaking at break-neck speed from second base.

We cannot see the face of the black batsman,
but the 42 on his back and his stance
tells us that this is Jackie Robinson,
skilled beyond anyone else in his day (and in ours)
in the art of the bunt.

Jackie is seen here
putting his technique to use
for a form of the hit-and-run
that only he could do:
a perfect bunt down the third-base line
that might enable his running teammate
to score all the way from second base,
and, possibly earn Jackie a hit, too.

Robert Riggs — a painter,
printmaker, illustrator
little known during his lifetime —
comes to bat more and more these days,
his pictures exploding in sports books.
He seems now one of those few
who understand the ridiculously gorgeous
power of bodies in action and in light.

Jacob Lawrence's *Strike*

Lawrence called his style "dynamic cubism."
In the dynamics of this moment
a ball passes a batter whose swing fails to hit it.

The ball, still in flight, is paused
a hair's breadth from its target, the catcher's mitt.
The white-uniformed stride of the batter,

and the powerful failure of his swing
fills most of the picture,
but at the heart of the scene crouches the catcher,

a black man getting this difficult job done in 1949
in an almost entirely white league,
his passion for the task

declared by the bright scarlet
of his protective gear and mask.
Though the batter, the next hitter, and the ump

are all of the Caucasian persuasion —
the larger dynamic here is the collage of faces
that crowd the stands behind the plate,

where we see almost as many blacks as whites.
We can assume that many fans have come to witness
the play of Roy Campanella, the great catcher,

a superstar playing under the same enormous pressure
as Jacob Lawrence, just returned from an asylum,
looking in '49 to regain his fame
with the perfect strike that is this picture.

Lisa Dinhofer's *Spring Street Hardball*

This tabletop still life has lots on its balls —
its four actual baseballs (two clean and two worn),
its three glass baseballs, its array of glass marbles
of many styles and colors,
and its crystal ball on a pedestal.

That last is the largest ball of all and —
with, perhaps, some deference
to the prediction of the future —
resides just above
exact dead center.

The lace tablecloth
on the bare-wood table
is a well-rounded cacophony, too,
of circular motifs that plays with the balls
for the sake of echo and embellishment.

The artist is an illusionist here
who makes every ball
meticulously real
within its own peculiar sphere,
but without concern for the reality of the whole,
so that the two rounded reflections

of Spring Street
can be, for the sake of the fun of it, upside down —
thereby seeming to be twin parodies
of Edward Hopper.

Dinhofer reflects on herself, too.
Her self-portrait in a glass baseball
rests on a blood-red doily —
likely a reflection on the game
as a long-lost passion.

She grew up in Brooklyn.

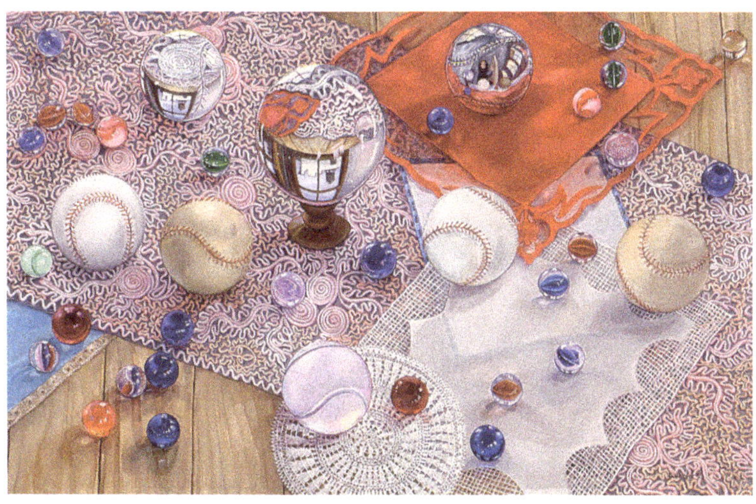

Lisa Dinhofer, *Spring Street Hardball*, 1988

Andy Warhol's *Baseball*

For Warhol baseball is
thirty-seven batsmen
all seen in profile,
all swinging mightily.
all Roger Maris —

the newsprint image
a product
of the infamous year
the long-suffering Roger
hit his sixty-one dingers.

As with Warhol's other
celebrated celebrity portraits
this grid of endlessly echoed actions
consists of one silkscreened
smear after another

so that this display of Rogers
appears to offer
subtle variations on a theme —
though, in truth, the variations
were products of accidents,

whatever happened when
Andy or an assistant
spread and distressed the ink.
Thus these seven rows of Maris
are meant to say nothing in particular

and all this repetition of swings
wins him no game,
makes him no icon.
This print gets Warhol museums
but Maris no halls of fame.

Andy Warhol's *Pete Rose*

To commemorate
Charlie Hustle's breaking
of Ty Cobb's record

a Cincinnati art dealer
commissioned this print,
the ultimate in baseball cards.

Rose looks striking and about to swing
at whatever we might pitch him,
his blazing white uniform

stark against a dark blue background,
a nightmare version of sky,
tricked out with blazing red details:

Pete's helmet, number, and name;
Cincinnati's signage and logo.
At the edge of this icon

a strangely broken, gold-tinted baseball
seems about to open its mouth
and take a bite out of Pete Rose.

Seymour Leichman's *Fate Takes a Hand*

According to Leichman the most marvelous
of the miracles of the Miraculous Mets in 1969
required intervention fated and divine —
an angel carries a horizontal
Ron Swoboda, he of the glove of stone,

towards an improbably (impossibly?)
skillful diving catch of Brooks Robinson's
line drive in the ninth inning of game four.
Thereby enabling the worst fielder
on the worst fielding team

to save the day by the niftiest of plays.
Behind the action the stands are filled
with a historical mix of uniformed Mets
and a cartoon-faced caricature of Leichman
laughing the happiest of happy-fan laughs.

On the Classic Photo of *Jackie Robinson Stealing Home*

it is so hard
        ideally the play is tried with two outs
caught in the middle
        and less than two strikes on the batter
between their hate and his fate
        left-handers using full windups
once begun he had to run
        provide the best chance
for his life
        you will need about four seconds
but he always said:
        to cover the distance
"above all else
        from leadoff to diving slide
I hate to lose"

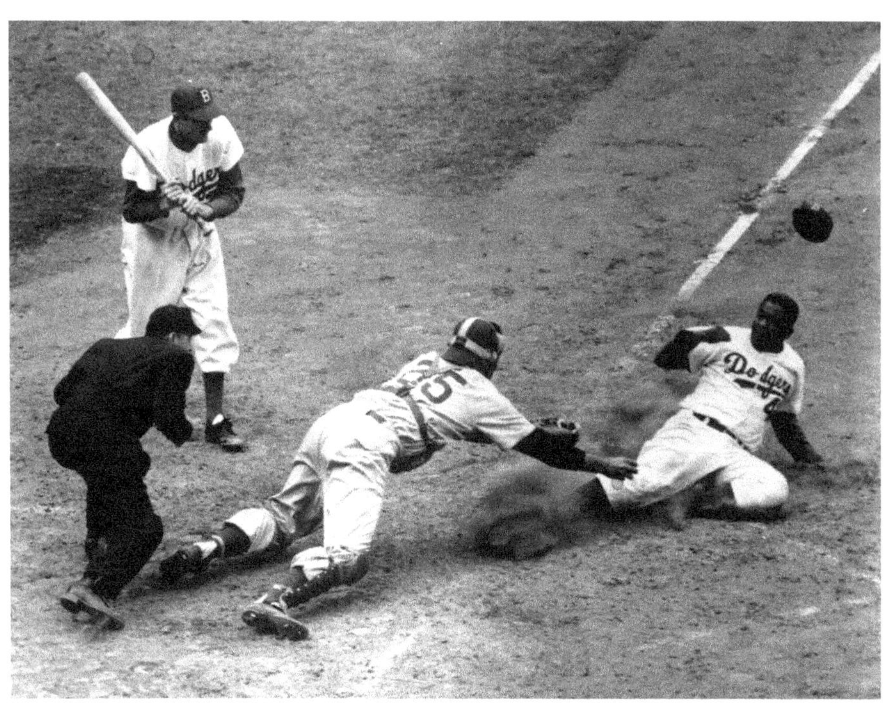

Jackie Robinson Steals Home Against the Chicago Cubs in 1952

Screens in the Dark

"We'll Always Have Paris": Years Later, Rick Thinks He Sees Ilsa, One Last Time, in Paris

"Last night we said a great many things."
This is a big intersection.
The avenues are wide
that come together here,
and he has seen cars,
buses, people, and bicycles
rub each other the wrong way.

"You said I was to do the thinking for both of us."
He has seen Parisians here
with noses interlocked,
hands on hips or waving in the air,
disputing an embrace of fenders,
oblivious
to belligerent honks and squawks.

"If that plane leaves the ground and you're not on it . . ."
Things come together here
and sometimes cross.
He sits at his usual seat
reading a book
or the characters that walk past.
This café is a union
of inside and outside.
He sits on the seam.

(continued)

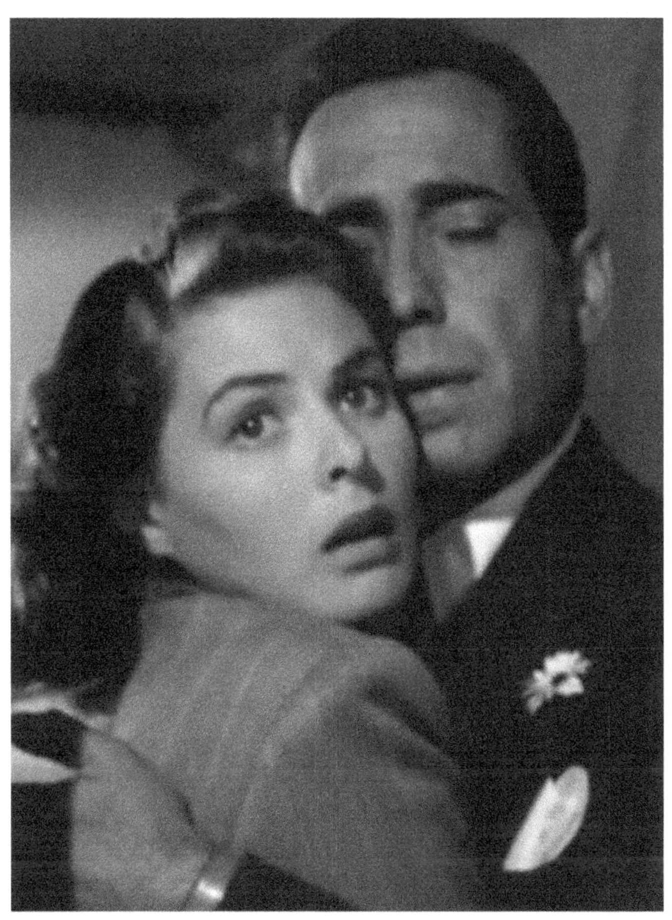

Ingrid Bergman and Humphrey Bogart in *Casablanca*, 1942.

“Inside of us we both know you belong with Victor.”
    Sometimes,
    on rainy days like today,
    he reads further inside,
    backwards from where his past
    almost intersects this moment.
    He descends, like Orpheus,
    on a half-remembered tune
    the rain strums.

“Here’s looking at you, kid.”
    Staring through water beading on glass,
    he tries to bring this scene into focus.
    A beautiful woman who resembles
    someone he used to know,
    or should have,
    is hurrying towards him
    from across the street.

“Where I’m going you can’t follow.”
    She is hugging a bouquet of white roses.
    Streams of familiar, amber hair
    flow from a pale pool.
    A smile ripples.
    Luminous eyes almost meet his
    before sinking
    into a subway entrance.

The Usual Suspects

A gathering of suspects might be
a way to solve a crime —
a heist, say, of a truckload of guns —
but a collecting of miscreants
might also be a scheme

orchestrated by the devil himself —
a fiend who, long ago,
murdered his wife and children
to deprive his foes of a means
to threaten.

"Who is Keyser Söze?"
The question's asked again and again
and we think we have no answer,
but we might have guessed
he's the one suspect left alive,

the one telling the story
we have been watching
with rapt attention
while missing the clues
that show

how little of what we know
is true.

Vertigo

A fear drops a plumb line,
Hitchcock's horrific zoom-in and track-back
to a depth hope cannot rise above.
But a falling can also be
into the madness that is love,
a vortex spinning down a mind,
whose bottom line
might be terrible to consider.

A portrait of Carlotta,
the beautiful Carlotta,
the sad, the mad Carlotta
could be a portal to the past
or a bad dream
of an old house on the corner of Eddy and Gough,
a grave at the Mission Delores with Carlotta's name on it,
a leap into the Bay at Old Fort Point out at the Presidio,
a fatal bell tower at San Juan Bautista,
a hundred miles down the coast.

But that peculiar bunch of flowers,
the twist to the hair, and the simple gray suit
are as real as the beautiful city of San Francisco
and the two cars, one white the other green,
that swing left, then right, then left,
pursuing each other for miles of film,
somehow always downhill,
the way everything must go,
it seems,
when desire overwhelms almost everything,
except for death itself,
viewed from the highest vantage,
vertigo overcome at last,
as Midge's dearest Johnny-O stands above,
finally fearless,
out on the ledge of the world,
with no one left to save,
no one left to love.

Yojimbo

Into a box of malevolence pretending to be a town
an indifferent, muscular swagger strides.
Across the ronin's path scampers
a scrawny dog with a human hand
clutched in its jaws,
and we know we have entered a kind of hell,

a place where we see
two factions seek
the nameless samurai's ferocious skills,
as he plays the gangs,
one against the other —

watching them,
aloof in the town tower
or aside in the sake shop —

as the rival evils
kill and kill
until, to the last man,
they kill each other
off.

Rashomon

Rape and murder can go round and round,
but the telling might be a dead end.

This tale is sunlit, but we see it told
in torrential, cinematic rain.

Do we believe the woodcutter's first story that seems,
an unbiased account, a simple outline of facts?

Can we bow to the bandit's yarn bristling as it is with
   persuasive specifics
but compromised by an absurdly brandished braggadocio?

Should we accept the wife's shame-faced admissions
just because they are so self-condemning?

What of the dead man's testimony so bitter and enraged?
Does his speaking from beyond the grave make his words
   more reliable? Or less?

Can we believe the woodcutter's second tale in which
   all are cowardly,
and the woodcutter himself a thief?

In penultimate despair the priest, our ultimate witness
   of the witnesses,
loses faith,   until a baby cries

and Kurosawa allows the priest, and us, to find
one man, at least, who transcends, despite his lies.

D.O.A.

I want to report a murder.
Who was murdered?
I was.
So begins a film and concludes a life.
A noir *memento mori*:
the dead man's telling of his tale
is what the movie is.

Frank Bigelow, an ordinary man,
a no-account accountant
an un-notable notary
has notarized
a bill of sale that,
unbeknownst to most,
makes him witness to a crime,
about which he has no clue,
but, this being noir,
he must find out,
and he does,
investigating his own murder
and killing his own killer.

This is also about jive
in San Fran night life,
and big buildings in LA
with forbidding façades
and long dark hallways
down one of which Bigelow
walks his last walk,
with us following
his walking, walking, walking
till he gets to the door that says
HOMICIDE.

Don't Look Now

The child of your heart,
the thing you hold most dear,
could be just around the corner,
just out of view, running,

a slicker scarlet bright,
the loved one
you long so much to see again,
so long now overdue,

unlike your death
that must arrive,
so very regrettably,
right on time.

Being John Malkovich

To be or not to be
the me or he or she
that she or he or me
would like to be

could be a ride inside
where, through a portal,
we see, *really* see,
through some other guy's eyes and mind,

an inner view
where a lost artiste seems to find
his elixir; his Faustian wine;
his silly, dark desire

so that he can try
to take to heart a self
that is not, after all, himself,
plucking strings to play,

a complicated part,
above or beyond the heads of all,
where all that living is
is puppetry.

Eternal Sunshine of the Spotless Mind

His Eve has tempted him
to take a bite of the fruit
of no knowledge of her,
and now Joel is trapped
in the slow digestion
of the poisoned apple
that is his life.

A witchcraft
aims to leave him,
as in a dream upon waking,
entirely healed
of his hope's imperfections.

But he tries and tries
to hold still in mind,
his imperfectly divine someone,
though she's disappearing all the time,
even as he withstands, as best he can,
this dark night's inexorable machine
of erasure.

And we are caught —
as we watch Joel striving,
in the face of the scrims and dissolves
of outrageous excision,
to hold onto his,
oh, so darling Clementine,
and we are there with him,
clinging to whatever Montauks
still remain
to us.

The Seventh Seal

Jof's last vision has to be
the ultimate revelation,
the etched scene
that provoked the film,
Death at his antic Dance,
le danse macabre, der Totentanz,
the theme of so many medieval prints,

folk of all stations swaying to
the apocalyptic swing tune,
a jig that strums *memento mori*,
plucked by the grim reaper's
taut, invisible strings,
arrayed for us through Jof's eyes,
silhouettes along a grim horizon,

a horizon that is not, as it turns out,
the end of all,
but just one of those ends
we rejoice to have gone beyond,
departing with Mia and Jof
and their precious infant Mikael,
three sweet antidotes to darkness.

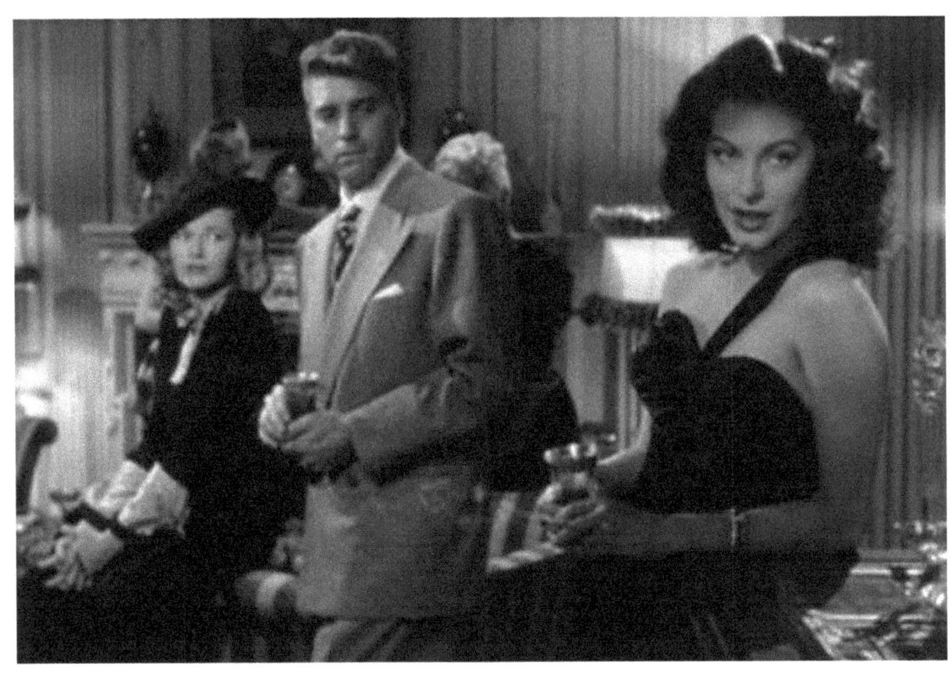

Ava Gardner and Burt Lancaster in *The Killers,* 1946.

The Killers

When you know they know where you are,
you know the killers will be coming,

with their long car and their short guns,
with their crisp, dark suits; their iron eyes.

Somewhere outside a bird warbles,
"there's-no-why, there's-no-why."

The Shawshank Redemption

Salvation might lie within,
even for innocent souls
whose dark night this prison is —
stacked blocks of cells,
words on a page of Dante's horrors

come by way of Stephen King,
a Purgatory perhaps,
too dreary to be a Hell —
a fate inescapable
until the much martyred
Andy ascends

from books in the basement
to pale ale on the roof
to Mozart in the air;
and then plunges,
erotic and Biblical,
through lovely Raquel
whose curves sing the music
of her spheres,
channeling Rita and Marilyn, too,
those other redoubtable cheesecake seraphim
of Andy's unexpected
transubstantiation.

To the startling Heavenly light
of Zihuatanejo
our narrator, Red,
must also make his way,
redeemed at last,
in spite of all his doubts,
by what an angelic Emily calls
"the thing with feathers,"
the thing
none of us,
no matter what our prison,
can entirely live without.

The Exorcist

Why would the devil want to snare
a child? Karras asks.
Merrin offers a guess:
I think the point is to make us despair.

Pazuzu: a stone statue,
a cinematic grimace,
a voice demonic and grotesque
(via Mercedes McCambridge).

We tremble at the rising bed,
the shaking room, the frozen air,
the spider walk, the twirling head,
the spinal-tap medical care;

but there sings beneath it all,
a rolling tinkle of tubular bells —
a melody so strange and beautiful
that it becomes the fear we feel.

It sings each time we watch the film,
a ringing dread for what's ahead, a tolling
that undertones a mother's thoughts
as she strides autumnal Georgetown —

alone, at peace, almost unsuspecting.

Groundhog Day

Some days threaten never to end,
but this one just keeps coming back again.
A song by Sonny and Cher,
a DJ's shouted, "It's cold out there!"
and Phil is off once more —
seeking, he realizes, Rita's love,

but finding only despair,
a February second
repeated *ad absurdum*,
the fairytale hero here
becoming his own
fairy godfather,

giving himself an offer
he must learn how not to refuse,
remaking himself a prince
with scant help from the kiss
that never entirely arrives,
though he seeks it so desperately.

Phil must make a magic moment
out of an odd redundancy of striving
to be better than he is —
though trapped, he knows,
in the not very original sin
of being a jerk at heart.

For all of us, this is
a transformation devoutly to be wished —
a joking way to say we can
eat our world and have it too,
avoiding our idiocy's
diminishing returns.

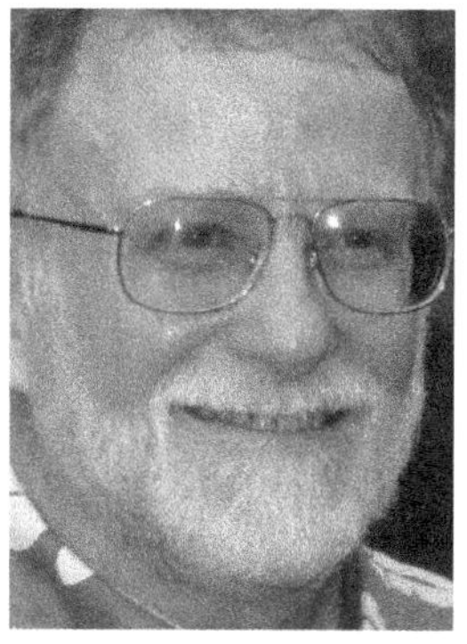

photo: Franklin Hayashida

About the Author

Joseph Stanton's previous books of poems are *Things Seen, Imaginary Museum: Poems on Art, A Field Guide to the Wildlife of Suburban Oahu, Cardinal Points: Poems on St. Louis Cardinals Baseball*, and *What the Kite Thinks: A Linked Poem* (co-authored with Makoto Ōoka, Wing Tek Lum, and Jean Toyama). His other sorts of books include *Looking for Edward Gorey, The Important Books: Children's Picture Books as Art and Literature, Stan Musial: A Biography*, and *A Hawai'i Anthology*. His poems have appeared in *Poetry, Harvard Review, New Letters, Ekphrasis, Antioch Review, Ekphrastic Review, Poetry East, Cortland Review, New York Quarterly,* and many other magazines. He has collaborated on many occasions with artists, musicians, and other writers. He has received many awards for his work — including the Tony Quagliano International Poetry Award, the Cades Award for Literature, and the Ekphrasis Prize. He is Professor of Art History and American Studies at the University of Hawai'i at Mānoa. He occasionally teaches poetry workshops, such as the "Starting with Art" workshops he has taught at Poets House and the Honolulu Museum of Art.

www.ingramcontent.com/pod-product-compliance
Lightning Source LLC
LaVergne TN
LVHW052353100826
845147LV00013B/833

* 9 7 8 1 9 4 7 0 6 7 8 5 1 *